THE STORM INSIDE

May 7
Single Mom's day

The Storm Inside

Trade *the* Chaos *of* How You Feel *for the* Truth *of* Who You Are

SHEILA WALSH
with Denise Wendorff and Karen Lee-Thorp

THOMAS NELSON
Since 1798

NASHVILLE   DALLAS   MEXICO CITY   RIO DE JANEIRO

Published in Nashville, Tennessee, by Nelson Books, an imprint of Thomas Nelson. Nelson Books and Thomas Nelson are registered trademarks of HarperCollins Christian Publishing, Inc.

All Scripture quotations, unless otherwise indicated, are taken from *The Holy Bible, English Standard Version*, copyright © 2001 by Crossway Bibles, a division of Good News Publishers. Used by permission. All rights reserved.

Scripture quotations marked NIV are taken from The Holy Bible, *New International Version®, NIV®*. Copyright © 1973, 1978, 1984, 2011 by Biblica, Inc.® Used by permission. All rights reserved worldwide.

Scripture quotations marked NKJV are taken from the New King James Version. Copyright © 1982 by Thomas Nelson, Inc. Used by permission. All rights reserved.

Scripture quotations marked NLT are taken from the *Holy Bible, New Living Translation*, copyright © 1996, 2004. Used by permission of Tyndale House Publishers, Inc., Wheaton, Illinois. All rights reserved.

ISBN: 978-1-4016-7763-3

Printed in the United States of America

14 15 16 17 18 19 RRD 6 5 4 3 2 1

Contents

About This Study

IF YOU'VE EVER LIVED THROUGH A TORNADO, hurricane, blizzard, or wildfire, you know that a storm can devastate a life in minutes. Treasured possessions are soaked, burnt, or torn apart beyond recognition. Sometimes the power goes out for days and you're left sitting in darkness.

Life can be like that. Our own choices or the things other people do to us can be equally shattering. The event may pass, but the storm inside goes on. Heartbreak. Fear. Regret. Insecurity. Shame. Despair. When these emotions churn inside us, it's hard to receive God's love or to love our neighbors as we want to.

God offers us a way through the storm. In *The Storm Inside*, we'll look at the stories of eight biblical women who traveled the path from shame to love, from disappointment to hope, from insecurity to confidence, from despair to faith, and more. We'll get to know them as real people and see how God came through for each of them. We'll see the crucial choices they made, and we'll lay hold of the grace that forgives what is past, gives strength for the present moment, and offers hope for the future.

These were women who would often be overlooked or despised — a prostitute, a destitute widow, an orphan — but God stepped into their lives, changed them, and gave them roles in accomplishing His purposes. He wants to do the same for you. Will you join me in discovering their stories?

I'd love to stay connected with you throughout your journey. Be sure to visit www.sheilawalsh.com where you'll find additional resources and encouragement. We can also connect on Twitter @sheilawalsh and Instagram @sheilawalsh1.

Sheila Walsh

How to Use This Guide

Group Size

The Storm Inside video curriculum is designed to be experienced in a group setting such as a Bible study, Sunday school class, or any small group gathering. To ensure that everyone has enough time to participate in discussions, we recommend that large groups break up into smaller groups of four to six people each.

Materials Needed

Each participant should have her own study guide, which includes notes for video segments and group discussion questions, as well as personal studies to deepen learning between sessions. Although the course can be fully experienced with just the video and study guide, participants are also encouraged to have a copy of the book *The Storm Inside*. Reading the book along with the video sessions provides even deeper insights to make the journey richer and more meaningful.

What's Included

The Storm Inside includes:

- Eight group sessions.
- Five days of personal Bible study for use between each session. These studies track along with the video teaching and group discussion sessions.

FORMAT OPTIONS

The Storm Inside can be used by groups that meet for one hour or two hours. Each group session can be completed in one hour but includes optional activities and group discussions that expand the material to meet the needs of groups that meet for two hours.

TIMING

The time notations — for example, (17 minutes) — indicate the *actual* time of video segments and the *suggested* time for each activity or discussion. Adhering to the suggested times will enable you to complete each session in one hour. If you have additional time, you may wish to allow more time for discussion and activities.

Alternate time notations and optional activities for two-hour groups are set off with a gray background. For example:

PROMISE *(10 minutes)*

> *If your group meets for two hours,*
> *allow 20 minutes for this discussion.*

In this example, one-hour groups allow 10 minutes for the discussion and two-hour groups allow 20 minutes for the discussion.

FACILITATION

Each group should appoint a facilitator who is responsible for starting the video and for keeping track of time during discussions and activities. Facilitators may also read questions aloud, monitor discussions, prompt participants to respond, and ensure that everyone has the opportunity to participate.

PERSONAL STUDIES

Maximize the impact of the course between sessions with five days of personal Bible study. Setting aside 20 to 30 minutes a day for personal study will enable you to more thoroughly explore the lives of the eight women you're studying and deepen your own journey from storm into love, hope, and faith.

SESSION 1

From Shame
to Love

The Samaritan Woman

*For I am sure that neither death nor life, nor angels nor rulers, nor
things present nor things to come, nor powers, nor height nor depth,
nor anything else in all creation, will be able to separate us from the
love of God in Christ Jesus our Lord.*

Romans 8:38–39

SHAME IS ONE OF THE MOST HUMILIATING, weighty burdens that a woman can carry. Just thinking about the things that have shamed us can send us into a corner to hide. Don't worry—I'm not asking you to share your deepest secrets here. Instead, in this first session you'll hear about the shame I carried for years, and you'll see how an encounter with Jesus transformed a woman whose shameful past made her an outcast in her hometown. We don't even know her name, but the woman from Samaria became a compelling witness after she experienced the life-changing power of Jesus' love.

WELCOME *(5 minutes)*

Welcome to Session 1 of *The Storm Inside*. If this is your first time together as a group, take a moment to introduce yourselves to each other before watching the video. As you give your name, also share the following:

> What is one word, emotion, or picture that comes to mind when you hear the word *shame*? (Examples: heavy, rejection, someone covering their face, hiding in the dark, crashing my parents' car when I was a teen.)

VIDEO: FROM SHAME TO LOVE *(20 minutes)*

Play the video segment for Session 1. As you watch, use the outline provided to follow along or to take notes on anything that stands out to you.

NOTES

"Shame is life dominating and stubborn. Once entrenched in your heart and mind, it is a squatter that refuses to leave."—Edward T. Welsh

Guilt tells us we have *done* something wrong. Shame tells us we *are* something wrong.

Shame is not what you did but who you are.

Only Jesus can address the life-threatening weight of shame.

God's love is greater than any shame that has found us.

Christ offers us a new wardrobe: clothed in the righteousness of Christ.

The Samaritan woman became the first evangelist.

We are never freer than when we tell Christ the truth about the things that have weighed us down and exchange those for His overwhelming love.

GROUP DISCUSSION

VIDEO DEBRIEF (5 minutes)

> *If your group meets for two hours,*
> *allow 10 minutes for this discussion.*

1. What brought you the most encouragement in Sheila's teaching?

SHAME (20 minutes)

> *If your group meets for two hours,*
> *allow 35 minutes for this discussion.*

2. What are the differences between shame and guilt? Give an example of shame and an example of guilt.

3. Read John 4:4–30. What does the woman at the well have to be ashamed of? What shame does she carry as an individual? As a woman? As a Samaritan?

STUDY NOTES

Samaria (John 4:4). After the Israelites of Samaria had flagrantly disobeyed God for centuries, God allowed the Assyrians to conquer their country and send many of their people into exile. The Assyrians moved conquered people from various other countries into Samaria to resettle the land. These people intermarried with the remaining Israelites and created a religion that was a mix of Israelite and foreign traditions. This is one of the primary reasons Samaritans were so hated by the Jews. They were viewed as a polluted people. See 2 Kings 17:24–41 for details.

Sixth hour (4:6). Noon. Drawing water and hauling gallons of it home was hard work, so women normally did it in the coolest morning hours. Only someone excluded from the company of other women would do it at noon in that hot climate.

Woman (4:7). At that time, no respectable Jewish man would talk with even a virtuous Jewish woman in public, not even his wife. A rabbi certainly would not discuss theology with a woman. This was in keeping with practices throughout the Middle East, where women were supposed to be as unnoticeable as possible in public and were discouraged from leaving the house except when necessary.

4. How does Jesus expose the woman's shame at various points in their conversation?

5. How would you describe Jesus' attitude toward her shame? For instance, does He suggest that she's fine and has nothing to be ashamed of? That she's unworthy of His notice?

As Edward T. Welsh says, "Shame is a squatter, staying with an unwillingness to leave." We hide our shame, embarrassed about who we are. We might share our guilt, but shame stays tucked away in the dark places of our life.

6. If you feel comfortable doing so, share about a time when shame invaded your life. Take a few minutes and have a couple of people share their story.

OPTIONAL GROUP DISCUSSION (20 minutes)
NOTICED

- After Jesus first speaks to the Samaritan woman, what thoughts and emotions do you sense behind her words in John 4:9? For instance, does she seem shocked, offended, friendly, hostile, bored, honored? Explain.
- Why do you think she continues to resist Jesus in verse 11?
- After what Jesus says to her in verse 18, why do you think she changes the subject to theology in verses 19–20?
- What are some things people do when their shame is exposed? What are some things they do when they're afraid their shame will be exposed?
- Have you ever had someone extend a hand to you in spite of your shame? If so, how did it affect you?

No SEPARATION (*10 minutes*)

> *If your group meets for two hours,*
> *allow 25 minutes for this discussion.*

7. In John 4:4–26, where do you see Jesus treating the Samaritan woman with love? List each instance, and tell how it reflects love.

8. In Romans 8:38–39, the apostle Paul makes a list of things that can't separate us from the love of God. What would you add to Paul's list? What are some things you sometimes fear could separate you from God's love?

9. It is impossible to get beyond God's loving reach. What comfort does this give you in knowing that God's love through Christ transcends any shame that you may feel?

As Paul says in Romans 8:38–39, nothing—not even shame—separates us from the love of God. Jesus pursues us, loves us, and steps across cultural lines to offer the gift of eternal life. As you close this session, bring your heart before God in prayer, using either the prayer provided here or your own.

Dear God, Your love is abundant and eternal, transcending all shame. You know everything I've ever done and everything others have done to me, and You sent Your Son to remove the shame of those things. In You I am clean and pure, with nothing to hide. Please help me to come out of hiding and trust Your love, and to treat others with that same shame-cleansing love. In Jesus' name, Amen.

[handwritten: woman at well - at least married 5 times/lives w/ a man]

[handwritten: he was alone, A well at noon]

BETWEEN NOW AND THE NEXT SESSION

Each session in *The Storm Inside* includes a week's worth of personal studies to encourage you and help you to make progress between meetings. In the studies this week, you'll look more closely at the Samaritan woman's story to see how she became a person who gave up her shame for Jesus' love. Will you consider setting aside 20 to 30 minutes a day for grace-based personal study? It's an investment that promises to yield significant returns. Don't miss out!

[handwritten notes:]

4 Truths

1. Jesus chooses the most unlikely people". Drawing water for the whole family) slave. Samaritan

2 "unexpected" - God speaking. points u in the right direction

3. picks us at our worst

4. shame is a liar
Guilt is a friend
• something I've done
• something done to me.

Never forgotten who I am w/ Him.

SESSION 1

When I regonize it
SHS by the well & waits for us.

PERSONAL STUDIES

DAY 1
PERSISTENT LOVE

Ted talks
Shame – it is not

> God's love is greater than any shame that has found us.
>
> *Sheila Walsh*

In Jesus' encounter with the woman at the well, He broke three Jewish customs: first, He spoke to a woman; second, He associated with a Samaritan, a group the Jews traditionally despised; and third, He likely drank from her water jar, which would have made Him ceremonially unclean. This persistent love startled even His disciples. Jesus persists with love that has no bounds.

1. When was the first time Jesus initiated His love toward you? How did He persist in order for you to hear? Check the boxes that relate to your love story.

   - ☑ Emotional need
   - ☐ Relational crisis
   - ☐ Culture
   - ☑ Shame
   - ☐ Addiction
   - ☐ Religious tradition

   - ☐ Moral corruption
   - ☐ Passivity
   - ☑ Health crisis
   - ☐ Intellectual pride
   - ☐ Loneliness
   - ☐ Other (name it): _____

2. How did you respond to His love when it was first offered?

Shame – I'm sorry I am a mistake

Guilt – I did something bad

3. Read John 4:4–30 again. How does Jesus initiate with the Samaritan woman? How does He pursue her?

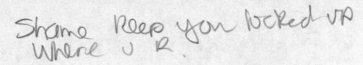

Shame keep you locked up
where u r.

STUDY NOTES

Jesus *had to* pass through Samaria (John 4:4). The region of Samaria lay between Judea in the south (where Jerusalem was) and Galilee in the north (where Jesus and His disciples came from). In Jesus' day, Jews traveling from Judea to Galilee did not pass through Samaria but went around the region on the east side of the Jordan. This took longer, but the Jews hated Samaritans. The Greek tense used here implies that Jesus was under compulsion from His Father to go through Samaria. He was on a divine mission.

Give me a drink (4:7). A Jew would become ceremonially unclean by using a drinking vessel given to him by a Samaritan. Anything a Samaritan had touched imparted uncleanness. He would have to perform purifying rituals before he could enter the temple.

---

4. Jesus crosses cultural boundaries to extend relationship to a woman. What does this tell you about His heart?

5. What does it tell you about the message of the gospel?

6. Jesus says, "Go, call your husband" (4:16), even though He knows the woman has no husband. How is it an act of love to expose her shame like that? Why not just treat her with kindness instead of throwing her sin in her face?

7. Has Jesus ever exposed your shame? If so, how did you respond? Did you take it as an act of love?

8. What evidence do you have that Jesus continues to love you, no matter what? (If you feel He doesn't love you, what causes you to feel that?)

Read Ephesians 3:14–21, where the apostle Paul prays that his readers will truly know the extent of Jesus' love. Use Paul's prayer as the basis of your own prayer, asking God to ground you in a solid awareness of His love.

> God loves us because of who he is, not because of who we are.
>
> *Phillip Yancey*

DAY 2
SHAME

> The bending of the mind by the powers of this world has twisted the gospel of grace into religious bondage and distorted the image of God into an eternal small-minded bookkeeper.
>
> *Brennan Manning*

1. Is there any thread of shame deeply embedded in your life? Anything you believe God is keeping track of in His bookkeeping? If so, what is it?

2. In a few brief words, describe your identity. Be honest: As you wake up in the morning and look in the mirror, how do you see yourself? What is your primary identity? Some examples:

   My family defines me. I am my husband's wife, my children's mother. Or, I am childless, divorced, never married, widowed, etc.

   My job defines me. I am what I do for a living, which is . . .

   My worst trauma or most shameful act defines me. I am an abused child, an adulterer, a thief, etc.

   My illness defines me. I have cancer, MS, bipolar disorder, etc.

I am a child of God, created as God's workmanship, created for good works that only I can do.

I am a broken woman, struggling to walk in my identity as a child of God.

I am an addict, struggling through life every day.

I am a woman with faith, but not that valuable to God.

I am a woman God loves.

3. When you define yourself, is shame part of the definition? If so, how?

4. Based on John 4:4–26, how does the Samaritan woman perceive herself?

5. How does Jesus seem to perceive her?

6. When we place our faith in Christ, what does Jesus do with our past and the sin and shame we carry around? Read the verses below and ask God to impress these truths upon you.

Isaiah 43:25

He blocks out transgressions for my own sake, and will not remember thy sins

Isaiah 44:22

Blotted out as a thick cloud thy transgressions, I have redeemed thy,

Psalm 103:12

As far as the east is from the west, so far hath He removed r transgressions from us.

Micah 7:19

He will cast ur sins into the seas He will return again

Acts 10:15

what God has cleansed, that call not that common

Hebrews 10:17

And their sins and iniquities will I remember no more

STUDY NOTES

What God has made clean (Acts 10:15). Here, God speaks to the apostle Peter in a vision. God is preparing Peter to take the news about Jesus to some non-Jews. Until now, Peter has assumed that Jesus is the Savior for Jews only, not for Gentiles and Samaritans. So God gives Peter a vision in which He commands Peter to eat food that is unclean by Jewish law, food that Gentiles eat.

I will remember (Hebrews 10:17). The writer is quoting Jeremiah 31, which promises a new covenant between God and His people. The writer is saying that Jesus' death and resurrection have brought about that new covenant. It guarantees that sins will be completely forgiven, with no additional sacrifice for sins needed.

7. How easy is it for you to fully receive God's promise that you are clean and your shame has been completely taken away? Why?

I am so A believer, I couldn't live if I didn't believe/receive God's promise

8. In John 4:28, the woman from Samaria finally understands that Jesus is the Messiah. Trusting in Him, she realizes that her past life has no bearing on the potential of her future. Her life isn't about what she did, but the hope of what Christ will do for her. Where do *you* need to recognize the forgiveness and cleansing of Jesus and walk in the realization of His love? Is it with regard to something you've done or something done to you?

Yes!!

27

Take some time to pray, releasing any shame and receiving the forgiveness that Jesus offers. Don't be ashamed to tell God exactly what you've been through and what you're feeling. If you have trouble believing you're forgiven or cleansed, tell Him so, and ask Him to help you know for certain that what is past is past. ✓

> Jesus did not identify the person with his sin, but rather saw in this sin something alien, something that really did not belong to him, something that merely chained and mastered him and from which he would free him and bring him back to his real self. Jesus was able to love men because he loved them right through the layer of mud. ✓
>
> Helmut Thielicke

Day 3
Living Water

Jesus wants to give the Samaritan woman a gift that is beyond her comprehension. He offers satisfaction that goes beyond physical need to the heart of her spiritual need. Yet she has trouble understanding what He's talking about.

1. Read John 4:10–15 again. When you imagine "living water," what pictures or ideas come to mind?

   He is giving her salvation = in the form of water & the Holy Spirit.

2. How is "living water" a fitting picture of the Holy Spirit and what He gives us? What does this term tell you about the Spirit?

   God loves us for who we are now and not who we were then, faith.

STUDY NOTES

Living water (John 4:10). This was the normal figure of speech for flowing water—as in a stream, river, or ocean—as opposed to still water in a lake or bath. That's what the woman thinks Jesus means in 4:10–11. But He invests the expression with deeper meaning.

In John 7:37–39, Jesus speaks of living water again, and John says it refers to the Holy Spirit. Living water points to the Spirit and everything He does in our lives.

Gift (4:10). The Greek here emphasizes God's grace through Christ. Jesus gives life freely, as a gift.

Our father Jacob (4:5, 12). The grandson of Abraham. God gave Jacob the name "Israel," and Jacob became the father of the twelve tribes of Israel. He was thus an extremely important ancestor claimed by both Jews and Samaritans. "Respect for the past prevented [the woman] from seeing the great opportunity of the present."[1] Also, she may have been trying to increase Jesus' respect for her by showing her knowledge of Jacob.

3. In verse 14, Jesus calls the Spirit "a spring of water welling up to eternal life." How is "living water" a fitting picture of a source of eternal life?

Living water is God's way of let the past go Repent & know God has forgiven you

4. Why do you think it's hard for the woman to understand what Jesus is offering? Where is her focus?

> She is not understanding what Jesus is offering her and does not want to be misunderstood.

5. How do you interact with Jesus? Do you tend to relate with Him primarily about your physical needs (finances, food, etc.)? Do you ever ask Him to satisfy the deep needs of your soul?

> No, but I will pray that now. mostly pray for my family, health safety.

6. If a person has a spring of life welling up inside her, do you think that should mean she will always feel good? What do you think the experience of living water should be?

> Everyone has times of need.

7. In Jeremiah 2:13, God rebukes His people for ignoring Him, the fountain of living water, and instead trying (and failing) to make their own cisterns to hold water. Do you tend to rely on your own resources rather than seeking the Holy Spirit to quench your thirst? If so, how do you do that?

> I rely highly on the Holy Spirit, but I also rely on myself, friends, family.

Spend some time thanking Jesus for His living water. If you're thirsty, seek Him to quench your thirst. If there are other things you do to quench your inner thirst, confess those.

> *Jesus, Your Holy Spirit is living water — a source of life that is abundant and overflowing. I look to so many other things to fulfill me rather than going to You. I come to You, the well of living water, and I ask You to fill me and satisfy my thirst. All forgiveness and satisfaction are in You. In Your holy name, Amen.*

Day 4
The Messiah

At the end of her conversation with Jesus, the Samaritan woman learns that she is talking to the Messiah. Let's look at the conversation that leads up to this realization.

1. Jesus knows that in order for this woman to place her faith in Him, she has to acknowledge her need for a Savior. In John 4:15–26, how does He help her face her need for a Savior?

   He said I know the Messias is coming Christ. Jesus said "It is he"

Study Notes

This mountain ... Jerusalem (John 4:20). The law of Moses emphasized that sacrifices and religious observances must be done "in the place that the LORD your God will choose" (Deuteronomy 12:18). The temple in Jerusalem became that place. But after the death of King Solomon, the northern tribes of Israel rejected worship in Jerusalem and set up alternate places, first at Dan and Bethel and later at Mount Gerizim. The site of true worship became a bone of contention between Jews and Samaritans, and the Samaritan woman uses it to change the subject when Jesus addresses her marital history.

In the Spirit and in truth (4:23). Jesus declares that under the new covenant, neither Samaria nor Jerusalem will be the focus of worship. Genuine worship will be inspired by and submitted to the Holy Spirit and to Christ, who is Truth and the source of truth (John 14:6, 15–17).

2. How do you think we can tell if our worship is in the Holy Spirit and in truth? Or how can we tell if it isn't?

I'm not sure. I just believe
in the Holy Spirit and use him as
a guide.

STUDY NOTE

Messiah (4:25). The woman has no idea what worship in the Spirit and in truth means, so she deflects the conversation again, to the vague future when the Messiah will come. The Samaritans were looking for an anointed prophet like Moses, but because they rejected all of the Old Testament books after Deuteronomy, they did not accept any of the predictions about the Messiah in the books of the Old Testament prophets. Nor did they accept the common view among some Jews that the Messiah would be a warrior king who would overthrow Rome.

---

3. The woman doesn't know much about the Messiah, but what does she know (4:25)?

Shame keeps me from
be fully emersed —

4. Jesus has prevented both demons and His own followers from telling people that He is the Messiah (Mark 1:21–25, 34, 40–44; 8:27–30). He has done so because He knows people have wrongheaded assumptions about what it means to be the Messiah. But here He acknowledges His

identity to this obscure woman. Read Mark 8:27–30 and John 4:26–29. Why do you suppose Jesus reveals His identity to this woman so plainly while hiding it from the crowds who follow Him?

5. Why do you think she doesn't dismiss His claim as crazy?

6. What is the disciples' reaction to seeing Jesus talking with the woman (John 4:27)? What is their main concern? What other concerns do they have (verses 31–33)?

7. In verses 34–38, Jesus states His priorities as Messiah. What are they?

From the beginning of His journey to Samaria, Jesus was compelled to a mission: an opportunity to share the gospel with a sinner, a time to reveal that He is the Messiah. Nothing got in the way of His mission.

8. Cultural barriers, religious traditions, geographic inconveniences—none of these mattered to Christ as much as "doing the will of him who sent me" and accomplishing His work. What keeps you from doing the will of the Father?

9. What helps you do the will of the Father?

10. Think about the people in your life who need to know Jesus. Make a list of those people, and spend some time praying for an opportunity to share the love of God with them.

DAY 5
LOVE SHARED

> Once we deeply trust that we ourselves are precious in God's eyes, we are able to recognize the preciousness of others and their unique places in God's heart.
>
> *Henri J. M. Nouwen*

The Samaritan woman begins this story in isolation, fetching water at the worst time of day in order to avoid her neighbors. Her encounter with Jesus cleanses her from shame and clothes her in love and righteousness. Her actions then demonstrate that her faith is real.

1. Read John 4:25–42. After Jesus tells the woman He is the Messiah, what does she do?

2. How do her actions show that she's changed from the way she was at the beginning of the story?

3. What has changed her? Why isn't she acting like a woman full of shame?

4. What happens because of her actions?

5. Jesus met with rulers and authorities, yet some of His most powerful messengers are people we would never expect, such as the Samaritan woman. How do you typically relate to those who need a Savior? Do you talk about Jesus? Do you feel embarrassed (ashamed) to do so?

6. Why do you suppose we so often fear rejection by people even though we have experienced acceptance by God?

Read Colossians 4:2–6, and make this your prayer. Ask God to guide you as you persistently show the love of Christ.

> Lord Jesus, I come to You devoted, praying that I would see more opportunities to speak about the mystery of who You are. I pray that love would invade every conversation I have. Help me to be alert, looking for people who are precious to You. Help me to not be put off by any stigmas or baggage they carry. I pray that my words would be like salt, perfectly seasoned, so that I would know how to speak to each individual.
>
> God, I pray that Your love would invade the hearts of those who need you. Make me Your messenger. In Jesus' name, Amen.

You are the heir to the kingdom. Prosperity is your birthright and you hold the key to more abundance in every area of your life than you can possibly imagine.

Henri J. M. Nouwen

From Disappointment to Hope

The Woman with the Issue of Blood

We can rejoice, too, when we run into problems and trials, for we know that they help us develop endurance. And endurance develops strength of character, and character strengthens our confident hope of salvation. And this hope will not lead to disappointment. For we know how dearly God loves us, because he has given us the Holy Spirit to fill our hearts with his love.

Romans 5:3–5 NLT

WHEN THINGS DON'T GO as we had planned and prayed for, when our expectations are unmet, we are disappointed. All of us experience disappointment. Albert Einstein failed his college entrance exam. Michael Jordan was cut from his high school basketball team. Charlotte Brontë was miserable as a teacher in Europe.

Disappointment isn't the end of the story, however. We can allow God to use it to form a life-affirming pearl, just as an oyster does when an irritating grain of sand gets into its shell.

In this session we'll meet a woman who faces overwhelming disappointment about an illness that has isolated her for twelve years. But she humbles herself and steps toward Jesus, believing in the hope that He offers to each of us.

WELCOME (5 minutes)

Before looking at this woman's story, take a few minutes to share the following:

When have you been disappointed, without the ability to change your circumstances?

there have been times

VIDEO: FROM DISAPPOINTMENT TO HOPE (18 minutes)

Play the video segment for Session 2. As you watch, use the outline provided to follow along or to take notes on anything that stands out to you.

NOTES

The level of disappointment we experience is measured by how much hope we have invested in the situation.

True

The greatest miracle the woman received that day was one she wasn't looking for and didn't know she needed.

Always the best Miracle's.

She wanted to be healed, but Jesus wanted to make her whole.

Indeed.

When the pain of remaining the same is greater than the pain of change, then we will change.

For sure.

We all have moments to step out or slip away into the shadows!

We do. Sometimes we just have to face our problems head on

The woman fell at the feet of Jesus, knowing her need of a Healer. She told Him the whole truth.

She did. He healed her. Praised her.

Jesus called her "daughter"—loved one, adopted one who belongs to Me.

Could there be a better feeling?

Are you held back by looking in the rearview mirror? Don't allow the disappointment of yesterday to rob you of the hope of today.

Sometimes. I pray a lot. Ask for forgivness - changed my way of thinking.

Are you defined by an issue or an identity?

No. They are all mine.

GROUP DISCUSSION

VIDEO DEBRIEF (5 minutes)

> *If your group meets for two hours, allow 10 minutes for this discussion.*

1. What brought you (encouragement) or a new insight while watching the video?

Mostly guilt n shame at first. Then I Didnt watch video. God helped me to forgive myself

DISAPPOINTMENT (10 MINUTES)

> *If your group meets for two hours,*
> *allow 20 minutes for this discussion.*

2. How would you describe what disappointment feels like?

To me... loss, failure, letting others down.

We must accept finite disappointment but never lose infinite hope.

Martin Luther King Jr.

3. Read Mark 5:25–34. At the beginning of this story, why is this woman disappointed? *She wanted healed.*

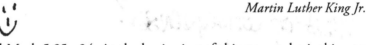

STUDY NOTE

Discharge of blood (Mark 5:25). The Greek phrase is *ousa en rhusei haimatos*, meaning "in a state of blood flow." This probably indicates a uterine disease. Today the condition would be called *menorrhagia*. Luke 8:43 says "she could not be healed by anyone." Mark 5:26 includes vivid details of her disappointments.

Leviticus 15:25–30 tells us more: bleeding made a woman ceremonially unclean, so that anyone she touched—anyone who even touched things she sat on—had to wash themselves and their clothes before they could enter the temple. She was therefore a social outcast. Her disease was considered shameful and disgusting. No respectable man would tolerate an unknown woman touching him in public, but he would be outraged if a bleeding woman touched him.

Seven days after the bleeding stopped she could be declared clean after making an offering at the temple.

4. Think of a time of disappointment in your own life. What effects did it have on your relationships with other people? With God? What other emotions did you have?

effect or consequences?
Hurtful to others
Shut people out who loved me.
Shame of being a person I didn't want to be.

HOPE (10 minutes)

If your group meets for two hours, allow 20 minutes for this discussion.

5. How does the woman demonstrate hope through action (Mark 5:27–28)?

She allows Jesus to help her heal —

6. In what ways is her action risky? What bad things could happen? (Notice in verse 33 that she is fearful when Jesus calls her to identify herself.)

She is fearful of the truth and thinking if he knew, she could not be healed.

7. If Jesus knows all things, why do you think He asks, "Who touched my garments?" (See verse 30.) What does He achieve by asking that He might not have achieved by pointing out the woman Himself or by letting her go unnoticed?

He knew who touched him — He wanted her to respond.

8. What do you make of the fact that just a touch of Jesus' clothing caused power to flow from Him? Should we think of this as magic, as something like plugging into an electric outlet, or as something else?

Christians believe it was His Holy spirit that ran through her.

OPTIONAL DISCUSSION (25 MINUTES)

PERSEVERANCE

- Read Romans 5:1–5. The apostle Paul says suffering produces perseverance. What is perseverance?
- Have you seen suffering produce perseverance and proven character in your own life? If so, describe how that has happened.
- Have you known people for whom suffering hasn't produced endurance? Read Romans 5:1–5 again. In the whole context of what Paul is saying, *when* does suffering produce endurance?
- If God is left out of the picture, what can suffering lead to? Why?
- What does Paul promise about hope in Romans 5:1–5? What is the source of our hope? What do we hope for?
- Is it possible for you to allow suffering to produce perseverance, character, and hope? Why or why not?

STUDY NOTE

Hope of the glory of God (Romans 5:2). *Hope* is waiting and long-ing for something we don't yet have, something we are confident we will have someday. God's *glory* is His shining, magnificent, awe-inspiring presence. Our destiny is to spend eternity in that glorious presence, where we will fully be who we were made to be.

We often pin our hopes on things God hasn't guaranteed. They may be good things, but they're much smaller than the glory of God. It isn't wrong to hope for things like healing from a disease, but we shouldn't confuse those with the greater things that God has promised us.

LIVING HOPE *(10 minutes)*

If your group meets for two hours, allow 20 minutes for this discussion.

Hope itself is like a star—not to be seen in the sunshine of prosperity, and only to be discovered in the night of adversity.

Charles H. Spurgeon

It's one thing to know hope intellectually and another to walk with faith toward the healing touch of Christ. The sick woman makes a definitive deci-sion to put her faith and hope in Christ.

9. When the woman comes out of hiding and publicly tells the whole truth to Jesus (Mark 5:33), what does she hope for? What does she get?

10. Take a few moments of silence to write down one or two of the things you most long for. Then ask yourself how much of your hope is focused on Jesus and how much on other people or things.

• forgiveness
• love –

11. What goes through your mind when you think about coming out of hiding and publicly telling the whole truth to Jesus?

I have told my whole Truth to Jesus. He Knows.

Ask your group to pray about the situation in which you've experienced disappointment, or about the thing you long for. Ask God to strengthen you through your process of perseverance. After praying, if time permits, watch online or sing the Hillsong United worship song "Oceans (Where Feet May Fall)."

Father, I stumble and fall in disappointment. My soul grows weary. There are things in my life that drain me of all vigor and strength. I put my hope in You. I cry out to You. I step toward You, believing in Your healing touch. I wait on You, aligning myself with Your sovereignty, timing, and will. Help me, Lord, to run with endurance. Fill my heart with the confidence of Your love that comes from Your Holy Spirit. I want to come out of hiding, tell the whole truth, and place my hope wholly in You. In Jesus' name, Amen.

We got a talker—

PERSONAL STUDIES

DAY 1
THE TOUCH

This "impure" woman is determined to touch Jesus' garment (Mark 5:28). According to the rules of purity, this touch will make Jesus unclean, rendering it impossible for Him to heal anyone else until He has been purified. What she is about to discover is that our brokenness never breaks Jesus, but His wholeness and holiness heal us. She is so desperate that she believes the risk and humiliation might be worth the potential reward.

1. What hope does the woman have in Jesus' garment in Mark 5:28?

    She believe any touch of His Clothes may be able to heal her

2. The woman tried everything in her own power—remedies, doctors, and all her resources. Where do you go for ultimate hope and healing? To Jesus? To other methods based on your own effort?

    Now a days. I go to God first (I hope) and family & friends later. I pray.

46

STUDY NOTE

Healing in its wings (Malachi 4:2). Malachi prophesied that the "sun of righteousness" (the Messiah) would come with healing in His "wings." The Hebrew word for "wings" could also be used to identify the tassels that Jewish men wore on the corners of their robe. Based on this prophecy, the Jews expected the Messiah to have healing in His tassels.

As a rabbi, Jesus probably wore tassels on the corners of His garment. The Jewish practice of wearing these tassels developed from God's command in Numbers 15:38–39, "Speak to the people of Israel, and tell them to make tassels on the corners of their garments throughout their generations ... And it shall be a tassel for you to look at and remember all the commandments of the LORD, to do them."

3. What would stepping toward Jesus look like for you? For example, it could be going to church, telling your small group some truth about yourself, going to a recovery group, admitting your need for healing, or writing a letter of apology.

   So many things. Letting Jesus into my heart knowing I am forgiven.

4. In reaching toward Jesus, the woman risked humiliation and punishment. What are you risking if you courageously step toward Jesus in the way you've described?

   You risk all that you are now and all of what your people, family & friends think of you if they knew who you once were.

5. Read Isaiah 41:13. What does God promise as we step forward in faith?

He does. I believe that.

6. Because the woman's disease had social consequences, she didn't have the confidence to approach Jesus; she just hoped to touch His clothes from behind. Do you see yourself as important enough to Christ to bring your disappointment to Him? Why or why not?

I have brought everything to Jesus. He know my old self. He knows me now.

7. If the woman had just touched Jesus' clothes, been healed, and slipped away unnoticed, she might have thought she was accessing impersonal magical power, much as we access and use electrical power or the Internet. She might also have carried her shame home with her, even though the bleeding had stopped. Jesus offered her the opportunity to come to Him face to face, person to person. Why is it important to remember that when we reach out to Jesus, we are reaching out to a Person, not just a source of power we can use?

Believe! You have to know in your heart - Trust in your beliefs.

8. Read 1 Peter 5:6–7. Write out a prayer to God seeking His care and comfort.

Dear Lord, Please forgive me of my sins. Please keep my children happy & healthy. please protect us, heal us, love us. Please God, always know we love you & praise you. In Jesus Name Amen

DAY 2
FALLING DOWN

> She wanted to be healed, but Jesus wanted to make her whole.
>
> *Sheila Walsh*

The woman with the issue of blood shows profound humility in first approaching Jesus, but she takes it a step further when Jesus calls her out. Her immediate need was to be healed. Jesus had her eternal destiny in mind. As Sheila said, sometimes the greatest miracle isn't the one we are looking for or even know that we need but something greater.

1. At first the woman desires physical healing, but once she is healed, Jesus goes beyond the physical to her spiritual condition. In Mark 5:33, why is she afraid? *It appears she is feeling undeserving of this healing.*

2. Why do you think she prostrates herself in front of Jesus?

    insecurity, thinking He won't call on her, shame.

3. Read James 4:6. God promises grace to the humble. Why do you suppose He doesn't give grace to proud people?

    God wants us to recognize our faults, believe in Jesus to forgive if we repent or confess, and have some remorse or dignity in the process.

49

> ## STUDY NOTE
>
> **Fell down before him (Mark 5:33).** In the ancient Middle East, it was common to lie prostrate on the ground, or to bow with the forehead touching the ground, to show supreme humility before a king or other superior or to worship a god. Both the Hebrew word *hishtahawa* and the Greek *proskuneo* could be used for prostrating oneself to greatly honor a human (Genesis 42:6) or to worship God (Nehemiah 8:6). In 1 Chronicles 29:20, *hishtahawa* is used for honor given to both God and the king (ESV: "paid homage"; NKJV: "prostrated themselves").
>
> *Proskuneo* is often used in the New Testament for people's response to Jesus (for example, "knelt," Matthew 9:18; 15:25 ESV; "worshiped" NKJV).

4. In Western culture, people tend to think of political and religious leaders as their equals. It would be unusual for someone to bow, let alone to kneel or stretch on the ground, before a leader. How often do you bow, kneel, or get on your face before God in prayer or worship? Why? Does this say anything about how you view God?

   Not very often. Kneel. in church.
   Will try face time. :)

5. What do you think are some appropriate ways to express humility before God?
   - *Prayers*
   - *Behavior*
   - *Praise*
   - *Faith*
   - *Love*
   - *Obedience.*

6. Read Luke 17:11–19. Here Jesus heals ten lepers, and one of them responds differently than the others. What does he do? Why does Jesus value this?

With a loud voice, Glorified God and fell down on his face at his feet giving him thanks. And he was a Samaritan.

7. Think about your own life. Is there anything that holds you back from falling at Jesus' feet and demonstrating gratitude? If so, what?

No. I could do it.

Offer a prayer of humility and gratitude to God. Consider kneeling or another wholehearted expression that demonstrates humility and gratitude toward God.

DAY 3
TODAY

Don't allow the disappointment of yesterday to rob you of the hope of today.

Sheila Walsh

The tenacity of this woman is remarkable. After twelve years of bleeding, it would be so easy to give up on life. Hope, though, comes to her through Jesus. We too often allow our past disappointment to limit the hope of our future. If our future is not secured and satisfied in God, then we live consumed with ourselves, desperately trying to make life work.

1. The apostle Paul wrote the book of Philippians as he sat in prison, tormented by persecutors. Read Philippians 3:12–14. Where does Paul focus in order to prevent discouragement?

> *I press towards the High Calling of God in Jesus Christ.*

2. How can Paul's words help us deal with disappointment?

> *By doing the same.*

STUDY NOTES

Prize (Philippians 3:14). The winner of the Greek races received a wreath of leaves and sometimes a cash reward. The Christian receives an award of everlasting glory.[2]

Upward (3:14). Paul's ultimate aspirations are found not in this life but in heaven, because Christ is there (see also Colossians 3:1–2).[3]

---

3. What do you focus on to prevent discouragement? Does the hope of eternity affect your perspective? If so, how do you keep eternity in the forefront of your mind? If not, how do you react to the idea of focusing on eternity?

> *Eternity w/ God in Heaven is my Ultimate Goal.*
>
> *Absolutely.*

4. God provides hope—not wishful thinking, but a promise. Read 1 Peter 1:13, and write down the promise God makes to us.

Be sober n hope to the end for the Grace brought to you at the revelation of Jesus Christ.

5. Read 2 Corinthians 4:16–20. What hope does Paul offer that supersedes the past or present? *To whom u forgive, I forgive also.*

STUDY NOTES

Light momentary affliction (2 Corinthians 4:17). The afflictions Paul describes as "light" included imprisonments, beatings to the point of near death, shipwreck, robbery, and all of the hunger, cold, sickness, and other risks that came with backpacking for hundreds of miles across rugged terrain as he spread the gospel (2 Corinthians 11:23–33). All this went on for more than twenty years, after which he was executed, yet he thinks of it as momentary compared to eternity.

Eternal weight of glory (4:17). Paul's afflictions are not light compared with the comfort we would all like to have. They are light compared to the weight of the glory he looks forward to. *Glory* makes us think of brightness and indescribable beauty, yet God's glory isn't just some shimmery nothing but a solid, weighty magnificence. That's our destiny.

6. Are you currently dealing with affliction? If so, describe it.

Maybe. Praying now for my mom who is dying. Praying forgiveness for cutting her out of my life for so long.

7. What difference does the eternal hope offered in Philippians 3 and 2 Corinthians 4 make to you in your current situation?

Gives me hope.

Have an honest talk with God about the affliction you're dealing with and the hope He offers. If you're having trouble trusting in what is unseen, tell Him that. Ask Him to help you have confidence in the eternal weight of glory awaiting you.

God is the only one that can make the valley of trouble a door of hope.

Catherine Marshall

DAY 4
JESUS' HEART

Mark sandwiches the story of the bleeding woman in the middle of a story about another healing (Mark 5:21–43). Mark intends his readers to compare the two stories. The contrast between the two is significant, yet Jesus' heart to heal is compelling in both. He does not neglect the needs of a desperate woman in order to save the daughter of a prominent religious leader.

1. Read the story of Jairus in Mark 5:21–24, 35–41. How does Jairus approach Jesus? What does he ask Jesus to do?

STUDY NOTES

Jairus (Mark 5:22). He was a synagogue official ("one of the rulers of the synagogue") with administrative responsibilities that included looking after the village's place of worship and watching over worship services. Sometimes the title was honorary and administrative duties were set aside.

By this time in Jesus' ministry, many of the religious leaders did not think well of Him. When Jairus approached Jesus, he took a huge risk. We don't know if he believed Jesus was the Messiah, but he knew Jesus had the ability to heal.

Made you well (5:34). The Greek word is *sesoken* (root: *sozo*), which can mean "healed" or "saved." Here both physical healing and theological salvation are in mind. In Mark's gospel, the two go closely together (compare 2:1 – 12).[4]

2. Jesus agrees to go with Jairus, but on His way He is confronted with the desperate, bleeding woman. How does Jesus deal with this situation? Is it a momentary delay, or does it take some time? How?

   He calls out to her to reveal herself.

3. What are the differences between Jairus and the woman in terms of social status?

   Jairus – was a signified official. She was just a Samaritan woman searching for healing.

4. What does Jesus' way of dealing with each of them say about Him? Why doesn't He give priority to the person with higher status?

God doesn't work that way Humble is the way He wants you to be.

5. Do you tend to give better attention to some classes of people than others? If so, which groups are you more inclined to pay attention to? Which are you less inclined to attend to?

I'd like to believe that I treat people the way I treat me or better. Like to say Always the Same. Not true

6. Because Jesus stops to heal the woman, people from Jairus's house tell Him that it's too late, his daughter is dead (5:35). How does Jesus respond (5:36)?

God Knows its never too late Faith in His ability to Heal.

7. What role does faith play in these two healings?

Faith is everything!

8. Jesus asks for one thing: faith. Faith in His ability to heal, faith in Him as the Messiah, faith that He can do anything. He asks not just for mental assent to these ideas, but for the kind of genuine conviction that leads a person to act on what he or she believes. Have you placed your faith fully in Jesus? What would acting on that faith look like?

Showing Him w/ my Actions that my faith is strong — I am a believer. I am Humble unto Him.

56

What are you facing today that requires faith in Jesus' ability and willingness to act? Bring this area before Him in prayer. Surrender to His timing as Jairus had to do. Reach out to Him like the bleeding woman. He is compassionate and loving. He notices each of us.

> When he saw the crowds, he had compassion for them, because they were harassed and helpless, like sheep without a shepherd.
>
> *Matthew 9:36*

Day 5
Daughter

> The moment someone chooses to trust in Jesus Christ, his sins are wiped away, and he is adopted into God's family. That individual is set apart as a child of God, with a sacred purpose.
>
> *Charles Stanley*

In Mark 5:34, Jesus bids farewell to the woman and says, "Daughter, your faith has made you well; go in peace, and be healed of your disease." This word, "daughter," acknowledges her faith and adoption into the kingdom of God. As a Jew, she is one of God's chosen people. She took a risk and stepped out in faith, but what a reward she received! Other than the women who mourn Him at the crucifixion, she is the only woman in the New Testament whom Jesus addresses as "daughter." But Jesus also says God's true children are not those with Jewish bloodline alone, but those who love Jesus Himself (John 8:41–42). And Paul later declares that even non-Jews can be adopted as God's sons and daughters.

1. Why do you think Jesus publicly calls the woman "daughter"? What does that convey to her? To the others who are listening?

That she is family. That she is loved as a daughter would be.

Even before God created the world, He planned to adopt a people as His own family through the redemptive work of Jesus. From the beginning of time, it was in God's heart to adopt this woman.

2. Read Ephesians 1:3–10. What had to take place "in him" in order for us to be adopted (verse 7)?

> *He had to see her as a daughter as a people of his own family.*

3. Imagine Jesus in all His love and compassion, looking into your eyes, calling you "daughter," confirming your identity, and claiming you as family. What impact does this have on your life?

> *Yes.... I made Jesus happy. He loves me, I am family. I am His daughter.' Great Joy.*

STUDY NOTE

Adoption as sons (Ephesians 1:5). Paul likens our adoption in Christ to the Roman law of adoption. In Roman law there were four implications of being adopted: (1) The adopted person lost all rights to his old family and gained all the rights of a fully legitimate son in his new family. Legally, he got a new father. (2) He became heir to his new father's estate. Even if other sons were born, he was still a coheir. (3) The old life of the adopted person was completely wiped out. The adopted person was regarded as a new person entering into a new life in which the past did not exist. (4) In the eyes of the law, the adopted person was literally and absolutely the son of the new father. (Paul speaks of "sons" because the Romans didn't adopt females. But God does, and Paul means the word to include women.)

4. How do you respond to the idea that you are holy and blameless in God's sight?

I am Thankful everday!!!

STUDY NOTES

Holy (Ephesians 1:4). The Greek word *hagios* means set apart for God in order to reflect His purity. It is a matter of not simply imputed but actual righteousness.

Blameless (1:4). *Anomos* means "free from blemish," like the sacrificial animals presented on the altar.

---

5. God has a greater healing in mind than just one woman's physical healing. What is His purpose for adoption according to Ephesians 1:9–10?

We should be Holy and without Blame Him in love.

6. Being adopted into God's family changes our identity. We become family and heirs to the God of the universe. Paul says later in Ephesians 4:22–24 to put off our old pre-adoption identity and put on our new identity. Our identity affects who we are and how we live. We need to live as the holy and blameless daughters we truly are. How does this affect your choices and priorities?

Ask God to make you fully and deeply aware that you are His holy and blameless daughter.

Father, I receive Your adoption, the daily assurance and the eternal security of knowing that I am Yours. I pray that Your grace would fall on me like rain and my life would reflect the truth of who I am. Thank You for the security of being Your child and for the hope of eternity. I am overwhelmed with Your incredible and compelling love for me.

God, my prayer is that I live out what is true about me. I want to reflect my identity, to let go of my disappointment and place my hope on the upward call of knowing and loving You. In Jesus' name, Amen.

FROM FEAR TO JOY

MARY MAGDALENE

Peace I leave with you; my peace I give you. I do not give to you as the world gives. Do not let your hearts be troubled and do not be afraid.

John 14:27 NIV

OUR SOCIETY KNOWS A LOT about pleasure. It promises every citizen the right to pursue happiness. In Thomas Jefferson's day, "happiness" meant well-being, but for most people today it means little more than good feelings. So we chase good feelings and often miss what our souls truly long for: joy.

Joy is the sense that all is fundamentally well, regardless of circumstances. Mary Magdalene has it. She enters the gospel story in torment and becomes one of Christ's most devoted followers. His healing touch transforms her spirit and produces joy that not even the worst tragedy can overcome.

WELCOME (5 minutes)

In this session, we will discover how Mary Magdalene faced her fear and found true joy. Give each person a chance to share the following in one sentence:

When does fear surface in your life?

VIDEO: FROM FEAR TO JOY (20 minutes)

Play the video segment for Session 3. As you watch, use the outline provided to follow along or to take notes on anything that stands out to you.

NOTES

Mary Magdalene understood the enemy's brutality. She had been possessed by seven demons (Luke 8:1 – 3).

Even Christians need to put on the full armor of God to stand against the enemy's attack (Ephesians 6:10–20).

We can stand strong because we have not been left defenseless.

Mary had total devotion to Jesus. She knew that darkness is no match for His light.

At the cross, Mary knew the Master, but she didn't know the Master Plan.

No matter how things appear, God is still in control.

Mary didn't walk away from the cross.

"Woman, why are you weeping? Who are you looking for?" (John 20:15).

Mary was the first to witness the resurrected Jesus, the pivotal moment of history.

No matter how many battles we lose on this earth, we win this war. Our victory is sealed in the blood of Christ!

GROUP DISCUSSION

VIDEO DEBRIEF (5 minutes)

> *If your group meets for two hours,*
> *allow 10 minutes for this discussion.*

1. What did you learn from Sheila's teaching about Mary? What hope did Sheila bring?

Fear robs us of joy—we are unable to live with "what is" because of the "what might be."

Sheila Walsh

FEAR (10 minutes)

> *If your group meets for two hours,*
> *allow 20 minutes for this discussion.*

2. Review Luke 8:1–3. Before Mary experienced the healing of Jesus, she knew fear from the power and brutality of the enemy. What do you think her life was like before her healing?

STUDY NOTE

Mary. Probably a wealthy single woman, because Luke names her first among a group of women who accompany Jesus and His male disciples from town to town, paying the bills. After a background filled with demonic plague, her healing faith in Christ transforms fear into courage and joy. She stands with Jesus at His crucifixion while the men are in hiding. And in a society that gives no legal status to the testimony of women, Jesus chooses Mary Magdalene as the first witness of His resurrected body and a proclaimer of His message.

3. Have you ever experienced such intense fear? If so, what was that like for you?

4. How about fear that comes in everyday life? What circumstances or events increase your fear?

Joy and Peace (10 minutes)

> If your group meets for two hours,
> allow 20 minutes for this discussion.

Joy is a pervasive sense of well-being.

Dallas Willard

We often think of joy as an emotional high. We may picture it as someone jumping up and down and shouting for joy as her son scores the first touchdown of his life. It can be like that, but joy doesn't require boisterous emotions. "A pervasive sense of well-being" can just as easily lead to a quiet smile, a relaxed body, and warmth in our relationships.

Joy is closely linked to peace. In John 14:27, Jesus speaks of a peace that replaces fear, smokes out the enemy and his work, and transcends our troubles here on earth throughout eternity.

5. Read John 14:27. How does Jesus describe the peace He gives?

> ## STUDY NOTE
>
> **Peace.** Wholeness, prosperity, quietness, rest. "Peace be with you" was a common Jewish greeting, but in John 14:27, Jesus uses it in an unusual way. Knowing He will be arrested in a few hours and killed soon after, He speaks to His disciples about peace. This peace is "the salvation His redemptive work will achieve for them — total well-being and inner rest of spirit, in fellowship with God. All true peace is in His gift."[5]

6. How is Jesus' peace different from what the world gives?

7. How does His peace speak to the fears you talked about in questions 3 and 4?

8. Read John 20:10–18. How does Mary respond to Jesus in her fear?

9. What changes Mary's perspective and reaction? And does that change of perspective affect her actions?

10. How does Mary's courage inspire you to find peace and joy in Christ?

OPTIONAL GROUP DISCUSSION *(30 minutes)*

SEEKING PEACE

The world's gifts concern only the body and time; Christ's gifts enrich the soul for eternity.

Charles Spurgeon

- Read John 16:33. What does Jesus mean when He says He has overcome the world? How does that contribute to our peace?
- Read John 20:19 – 23. This takes place right after Jesus' resurrection. How is forgiveness related to the peace of Christ?
- Read Philippians 4:6 – 7 and Colossians 3:15. How does prayer help us live in the peace of Christ? How does thanksgiving help us? What does it mean to say that the peace of Christ surpasses all understanding?
- What are some ways people seek peace apart from Christ?
- Is your heart troubled today? If so, how?
- What might draw you into the peace of Christ? Prayer? Gratitude? Forgiveness? An awareness of Christ overcoming the world? Some quiet time to yourself? Something else?
- Are there things you've done to seek peace that haven't helped? If so, what are they?

Peace is not the absence of trouble but the presence of God.

J. Oswald Sanders

RECEIVING PEACE (10 *minutes*)

Read John 14:27 again. Then pray together as a group (use the prayer provided here or say your own), committing to the Lord the areas of your lives that produce fear and take away His peace and joy.

> *Jesus, we receive from You peace, not peace that the world gives but peace that surpasses all comprehension. Your peace sustains us and frees us from the dominion of darkness and fear that overcomes us. We give our fear to You. We look to You, Jesus, as our healer, our Savior. We look to You as the Prince of Peace, the Lord of Lords. We receive Your peace and joy eternally, the peace and joy we gain because of Your death on the cross. In Jesus' name, Amen.*

PERSONAL STUDIES

DAY 1
FEAR

1. Look at the categories below and check the areas where fear resides in you.

   ❑ Out-of-control circumstances   ❑ Loneliness
   ❑ Current crisis   ❑ Children
   ❑ Past   ❑ Habits
   ❑ Future   ❑ Addiction
   ❑ Sinful tendencies   ❑ Health
   ❑ Thoughts   ❑ Other: _____

2. Look back to Luke 8:1–3. What was Mary Magdalene's affliction before she met Jesus?

STUDY NOTE

Shevah. Hebrew word for the number seven, from the root word *savah*, which means to be full, to be satisfied. The number seven is used over and over in Scripture to speak of completion. This was the extent of Mary's demonic possession.

We can imagine the effects of a life completely demonized. The despair and darkness must have been haunting. This was the life Mary knew. She was alone, perceived by others as an outcast.

3. Think about the darkest moments of your life. Write down some thoughts regarding your days in darkness, or days in which you had no control.

4. Read John 19:17–25. Describe the fearful situation Mary Magdalene chooses to endure as she stands with the other women.

Study Note

Cross. Records of crucifixions show that often the victim's feet were nailed sideways to the cross while the body faced forward. Such a position created a twist of about ninety degrees at the waist. The unnatural position, growing thirst, exposure to the weather, some loss of blood, and impaired breathing contributed to a lingering and painful death. The tension on the arms prevented normal breathing, which caused the lungs to gradually fill with moisture. The victim drowned slowly in an internal accumulation of fluid. The action of the heart was seriously affected. Frequently a crucified man might live as long as thirty-six hours, in increasing agony, unless by exhaustion or dementia he finally lapsed into unconsciousness.[6]

5. What do you think is going through Mary's head as she watches her Savior crucified?

6. How do you think she has the strength to stay at the scene of the cross?

7. Read John 20:1. What fears do you think Mary has to overcome in order to go to Jesus' tomb?

> Fear in the life of a believer should be hunted down and killed without mercy. At any point you see, smell or sense fear welling up in you to where you're basing decisions off it, to where you're allowing it to seep into your relationships, you need to attack the root of it, which is a failure to trust God.
>
> *Matt Chandler*

8. Believing God's promises is crucial to removing fear. The truth of His Word has to confront the fear in our thoughts and actions. Look up the following verses about fear, and write down the security of God's promise.

    Psalm 23:4

Psalm 27:1

Psalm 118:6

2 Timothy 1:7

Psalm 115:11

Deuteronomy 31:6

Isaiah 41:10

9. Mary put her complete trust in Jesus. In your own life, what do you need to leave behind to Jesus' healing touch in order to step forward in bold faith? Spend some time in prayer about this. Receive God's grace and the courage that only He offers.

DAY 2
LIGHT

> Mary knew darkness is no match for His light.
>
> *Sheila Walsh*

1. Read Colossians 1:13–14. According to Paul, what have you been rescued from? What does that mean?

2. In practical, day-to-day terms, what does it mean to be in the kingdom of God's Son?

When Jesus healed Mary, she was brought into the kingdom of light. This light is a present reality as well as an eternal reality. When Mary received the grace of Christ, this allowed Jesus to have sovereign rule over her heart. This freed her — as it frees us — from the rule of darkness.

STUDY NOTE

Delivered (Colossians 1:13). In Greek, *errusato* means to liberate, save, or rescue someone from something or someone. Christians have been rescued from a "domain of darkness." That is, we have been rescued from a realm in which the powers of darkness make the rules and control what will happen to us.

3. Read Romans 8:31 – 39. What things attempt to separate us from the love of God (and from His light)? Make a list, and circle any items that seem relevant to your life.

At the sacrifice of His own Son, God gives us everything needed for life and godliness. Sometimes we view an area of our life to be the exception to God's love and light. We will face fearful circumstances, as did Mary. Our hope is in the incredible love of God, demonstrated on the cross. Nothing can separate us from that love.

4. Do you ever forget — or stop believing — that you've been rescued from the domain of darkness? Do you ever live as if darkness prevails? The Scripture teaches that God has brought you into the kingdom of light, a kingdom where you experience the fullness of His redemption. Where are you missing out on His fullness?

To read further on God's light, see:

Psalm 43:3

Psalm 89:15

2 Samuel 22:29

Isaiah 42:5 – 7

5. What do you feel when you forget or stop believing that you've been rescued? What do you do?

God has promised that He will be a lamp to our feet and a light to our path (Psalm 119:105). Sometimes our steps are one at a time, and we trust in the light that God brings step by step. As with a candle or flashlight, we may not be able to see around the bend, but God will provide the light for one step at a time.

Respond to God in prayer and adoration as you think about the darkness, His light, and the way He has rescued you.

DAY 3
ARMOR

Paul compares our fight for joy and strength to that of a soldier on the battlefield. Mary followed Jesus with joy and strength. How did she do it? What equipped her to stand against the repeated tests of darkness? How did she overcome circumstances that did not initially depict what she believed about Christ?

1. Read Ephesians 6:10–12 below. Underline the two commands Paul gives.

   Finally, be strong in the Lord and in the strength of his might. Put on the whole armor of God, that you may be able to stand against the schemes of the devil. For we do not wrestle against flesh and blood, but against the rulers, against the authorities, against the cosmic powers over this present darkness, against the spiritual forces of evil in the heavenly places.

2. With whom do we wrestle? What does Paul mean by "the rulers ... in the heavenly places"?

STUDY NOTES

Be strong in the Lord (Ephesians 6:10). The Greek verb suggests "let yourselves be strengthened" in Christ Himself. It's not a matter of being tough on our own, but of making a choice to seek and receive the strength Christ offers. "Be strong in the Lord" is in contrast to fighting the enemy in our own insufficient strength. By faith, we pull from the resources of heaven to face our fears and execute the battles of everyday life.[7]

The strength of his might (6:10). The same strength that raised Jesus from the dead.

3. If we follow Paul's two commands, what is the result?

4. Most of us do not approach our life with a soldier mentality. In what area of your life do you need to stand firm and put on the Lord's strength?

5. How is this area of your life a battleground?

6. Do you ever attempt to fight in your own strength? If so, how?

7. Review the armor of God in Ephesians 6:10 – 18. List the six pieces of armor that Paul instructs us to put on. Next to each piece, clarify its purpose in battle.

8. Choose one piece of armor. How do you need it in your current battle?

Paul tells us to pray with alertness. Spend some time praying about the battle that confronts you. Ask God for His strength. Are you equipped with the right armor to walk in victory? Where do you need to remain more steadfast?

DAY 4
DEVOTED

To devote ourselves is to give ourselves up to something, to set ourselves apart for a special purpose. Christ's grace moved Mary to devote herself despite the most difficult circumstances.

1. How does Mary Magdalene show her devotion to Jesus in these passages?

Matthew 27:50–56

Matthew 27:57–61

Matthew 28:1

John 20:1–18

STUDY NOTE

Curtain (Matthew 27:51). The inner curtain that separated the holy place from the most holy place in the temple. The most holy place was considered God's throne room where the blood of atonement was offered. The tearing of the curtain signified that Christ made it possible for believers to go directly into God's presence.[8]

---

2. What do you think compels Mary in her undying devotion to Christ?

3. What compels you in your own devotion to Christ?

4. Mary weeps at the empty tomb until Jesus says her name: "Mary" (John 20:10–16). Hearing that, she knows His voice and sees Him clearly. In what ways, if any, has Jesus become blurry for you?

5. What helps you hear and recognize Him? What has helped you in the past, or what might help you now?

6. Read Hebrews 12:1–2. In your words, what does it mean to "fix your eyes on Jesus" (NIV)?

Study Note

Fixing our eyes (Hebrews 12:2 NIV). Derived from the Greek word *aphorao*, which means to direct one's attention without distraction, to look, see, behold. It implies undivided attention to the Originator and Perfecter of our faith.

Devotion comes when we know to whom we are devoted. Once Mary regained her sight of Jesus, she then proclaimed His resurrection.

Spend some time rededicating your devotion to Christ. Pray about anything that blurs your vision or hinders you from a heart that is totally His.

DAY 5
Joy

When we are powerless to do a thing, it is a great joy that we can come and step inside the ability of Jesus.

Corrie ten Boom

Mary observes, devotes herself, serves, and yet is powerless other than in her hope in Jesus. As she faces painful and confusing times, she has no emotional security other than her faith in Jesus. She is a monument of joy because of Jesus' healing grace. She knows what He has done in her life, and she is confident of what He can do in the future. She finds no greater purpose than devotion to her Lord.

Several years ago, a woman had an eleven-year-old son who was hospitalized for over nine months. Occasionally friends would drop by to pray and give encouragement to the family. One day, in the darkest of times, God gave this woman joy through a visitor. Nothing had changed with her son, but God brought the promise of hope through the women who came to pray. She tells the story over and over today, testifying of God's tender care and concern. He gave her joy that was impossible without the Spirit working through people.

Like Mary and this woman, we too can experience joy because of our hope in Christ.

1. Name a time when the Spirit released incredible joy in you—an unexplainable joy and gladness. (If you've never experienced that, don't be ashamed to say so.)

STUDY NOTE

Joy. The Greek word *chara* means a source of true joy or gladness. Joy is not a fleeting emotion but a response from the heart that is founded in the hope of Jesus. Mary's joy was founded on the promises of Christ that will be fulfilled in the future. Kay Warren, in her book *Choose Joy*, says, "Joy begins with our convictions about spiritual truths we're willing to bet our lives on, and truths that are lodged so deeply within us that they produce a settled assurance about God." Joy is a fruit of the Spirit (Galatians 5:22). We don't produce joy ourselves, but the Spirit of God produces it in us as we stay connected to Him.

2. After Jesus appeared to Mary and the others, they were "afraid yet filled with joy" (Matthew 28:8 NIV). Why do you think they felt both fear and joy?

The secret to joy is to keep seeking God where we doubt He is.

Ann Voskamp

3. Read Matthew 28:8 – 15. How is the guard's response different from Mary's, and why is it different?

4. Romans 15:13 links joy with peace and hope. Read the verse and explain how all three things work together.

5. Read John 15:11 and fill in the blanks below.

   These things I have spoken to you, that _____ may be _____, and that _____.

6. Jesus gives us an incredible promise in John 16:20–22. What is His promise?

7. How can you experience more joy in your life? What steps could you take in order to give the Holy Spirit more opportunity to produce joy in you?

It is His joy that remains in us that makes our joy full.

A. B. Simpson

For the rest of her life, Mary carried with her the joy of seeing her Lord risen from the dead. Even when He was absent from her in body, nothing could take from her the knowledge that He had healed her, that she had been faithful to Him in the daily labor of the ministry, that she had stood by Him in His agony, and that He had spoken her name on that remarkable morning at the empty tomb. We don't know if her joy was vivacious or deep and quiet, but the early church honored her as a steadfast witness who had come from the darkest terrors into the light of joy.

SESSION 4

From Heartbreak
to Strength

Hannah

*Even youths shall faint and be weary, and young men shall fall
exhausted; but they who wait for the LORD shall renew their strength;
they shall mount up with wings like eagles; they shall run and not be
weary; they shall walk and not faint.*

Isaiah 40:30–31

HEARTBREAK COMES IN ALL SIZES. Remember when your first pet died? Remember when you were stricken over the loss of a loved one, or you found out you had cancer? These moments of heartbreak can cause us to doubt God's character.

Whether heartbreak happens in a single event or continues for years, it can drain us of the energy to keep trying. We can feel too weak to function at all, let alone to stride forward in loving God and others.

In the midst of heartbreak, God offers us the strength that raised Jesus from the dead. As we wait upon Him, He promises that He will mend our hearts and renew our strength. In this session we'll meet Hannah, an ordinary woman with a profound heartache because of childlessness. But with strength from God, she perseveres and becomes the mother of a great man: Samuel—a prophet, priest, judge, and kingmaker.

Welcome (5 minutes)

Before looking at Hannah's heartbreak and faith, take a few minutes to share the following:

Have you ever been heartbroken? If so, how did you react initially? How did you deal with it over time?

Yes, Not good in the beginning. Better over Time.

Video: From Heartbreak to Strength (18 minutes)

Play the video segment for Session 4. As you watch, use the outline provided to follow along or to take notes on anything that stands out to you.

Notes

"Heartbroken" means unimaginable loss, out-of-control grief.

We want to be able to impact a situation, but sometimes there's nothing we can do.

Does it ever seem like heaven is silent?

In Hannah's time, infertility made a woman worthless in her culture's eyes.

Hannah's secret was that she knew where to take her pain, even when God seemed silent.

Hannah discovered strength by surrendering her deepest heartache to God.

Hannah wasn't making a deal with God. She was surrendering to Him what mattered most to her in life.

Through total surrender to God comes amazing strength.

God understands the depth of our pain ... There is joy in worshiping in the middle of the storm.

GROUP DISCUSSION

VIDEO DEBRIEF (5 minutes)

> *If your group meets for two hours,*
> *allow 10 minutes for this discussion.*

1. What did you hear in the video that brought you encouragement, strength, or new understanding?

HEARTBROKEN (10 minutes)

> *If your group meets for two hours,*
> *allow 20 minutes for this discussion.*

God whispers to us in our pleasures, speaks to us in our conscience, but shouts to us in our pain. It is his megaphone to rouse a deaf world.

C. S. Lewis

2. Read 1 Samuel 1:1 – 18. Why is Hannah heartbroken? What has added to her loss and pain?

STUDY NOTES

Children (1 Samuel 1:2). In ancient times, barrenness was a tragedy and understood as a sign of God's displeasure. Every man wanted a son. Without a son, his name was not perpetuated and he had no heir. Childbearing was a woman's most valued role.

Worship and sacrifice to the Lord (1:3). Three times a year men were required to be at the sanctuary in Shiloh to observe the main religious festivals. Most likely this is the Feast of Tabernacles in autumn, as also mentioned in Judges 21:19 – 21. Festivals were times of celebrating God's blessing and abundance, especially at harvesttime.

3. Heartbreak causes us to grow weary and fainthearted. Share about a time when you were heartbroken. How did you express your grief? What did you do, or what was going on inside that you didn't show on the outside?

4. Hannah prayed passionately for a son. Have you ever prayed passionately for something for a long time and nothing happened? If so, how did that affect your relationship with God?

OPTIONAL GROUP DISCUSSION (15 minutes)
PROVOKED
- Why do you think Peninnah provokes Hannah?
- Elkanah gives Hannah double portions (v. 5). Why do you think he does this?
- How do you think Elkanah's action affects Peninnah? How do you think it affects Hannah?

WAITING (10 minutes)

> *If your group meets for two hours,*
> *allow 20 minutes for this discussion.*

5. From the start, Hannah's hope is focused on God. How does she indicate hope through her actions in 1 Samuel 1:10–18?

6. Read Isaiah 40:30–31. What promise goes hand in hand with waiting for the Lord? How does Isaiah describe the results of waiting?

STUDY NOTE

Wait for the LORD (Isaiah 40:31). Or "hope in the Lord" (NIV). "Wait" or "hope" here is the Hebrew word *qavah*, which means to hope or wait for expectantly. The literal meaning is to strengthen something (like a rope) by twisting or binding (cords) together. As we expectantly wait for the Lord, our heart is bound together with God, and there we find strength. Biblical hope isn't simply a feeling of desire without much confidence. It is confident, expectant waiting. In our instant society we hate to wait, but waiting is an essential feature of the strength God wants to bind into our character.

7. Why do you suppose it's so important to God that we learn to wait expectantly?

8. Sometimes we get weaker as we wait. Isaiah promises that we'll grow stronger as we wait for the Lord. What do you think makes the difference?

OPTIONAL GROUP DISCUSSION (15 minutes)

TURNING POINT

- In 1 Samuel 1:18, we see a physical difference in the strength Hannah experiences. When is Hannah's turning point?
- Can you remember a time when God gave you strength in the midst of heartbreak, without your circumstances changing? How did that affect what you felt and did?

ACQUIRED STRENGTH (10 minutes)

*If your group meets for two hours,
allow 20 minutes for this discussion.*

Waiting on God requires the willingness to bear uncertainty, to carry within oneself the unanswered question, lifting the heart to God about it whenever it intrudes upon one's thoughts.

Elisabeth Elliot

9. Hannah routinely went to the house of the Lord, three times a year, to honor Him and remember His care. These festive occasions most likely deepened her sorrow because of her own barrenness. Hannah had respect for God, yet internally she was not experiencing the transformational strength of His presence. It is not until she talks to the priest that Hannah visibly changes her countenance.

    Where do you go for strength? Do you typically lift your heart to God or to something else?

10. In what area of life do you need God to renew your strength and help you soar like the eagle?

11. Are you willing to allow the waiting period, when God weaves together a strong cord of your heart and His, to strengthen you and transform your heartbreak? Talk about your attitude toward this waiting period.

Pray for those in your group who have experienced heartbreak. Ask God to strengthen you through it.

Father, we are exhausted. Our strength is depleted as we wait and wonder if we will ever be strong again. We put our confidence in Your strength. We cry out to You as Hannah did, hoping that in this process, You will knit our hearts together and in that intimacy we will find strength. Help us, Lord, to renew our strength. Allow us to soar again like the eagle. We desire for our attitude to be changed. We want the desires of our hearts to be one with Yours. In Jesus' name, Amen.

Personal Studies

Day 1
Downhearted

Elkanah has the insight to observe Hannah and see her heart. Hannah's heart is so broken that it shows. He sees her behavior and asks, "Why is your heart sad?" (1 Samuel 1:8 ESV), or "Why are you downhearted" (NIV)?

Our heart is revealed through our attitude and actions. Once while grieving the loss of a loved one, I said, "This is too painful. I don't have time to cry and still carry on with the responsibilities of my life." A grief counselor responded, "You can grieve now and let your emotion out, or you can let it slowly leak out the rest of your life. Whether now or later, it will come out."

1. In 1 Samuel 1:7–11, how does Hannah reveal the state of her heart through her actions?

   She wept and wouldn't eat.

Study Note

Why is your heart sad? (1:8). The literal Hebrew is, "Why do you have a bad heart?" Hannah's heart is full of the bitter fruit of grief. In Deuteronomy 15:10, the same phrase is used when Moses instructs the Israelites, "Your heart shall not be grudging when you give to [a person in need]."

---

2. When you are downhearted, how do you typically deal with it? For instance, do you eat less? Eat more? Cry? Wear a happy mask? Pray? Avoid prayer? Talk to a friend about it? Watch television? Shop? Note any of these actions (and others) that describe you.

All of the Above.

3. God has so much to say about the condition of our hearts. In Jeremiah 17:10, God says He searches the heart and tests the mind. In Psalm 139:23–24, the psalmist asks God to search his heart. Read those passages. What does it mean for God to search your heart?

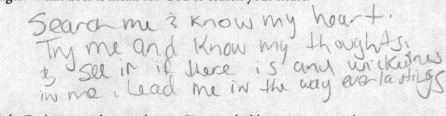

Search me & know my heart. Try me and know my thoughts. & See if if there is any wickedness in me. Lead me in the way everlasting.

4. Ask God to search your heart. Do you hold resentment or bitterness inside? If so, in what areas? If not, how would you describe the state of your heart? *Maybe years ago.*

5. If your heart holds resentment, how does this resentment play out in your life? Does it affect your interaction with others or your willingness to interact honestly?

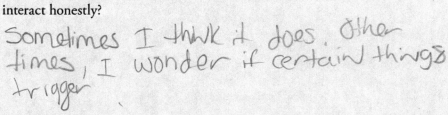

Sometimes I think it does. Other times, I wonder if certain things trigger.

6. In Hosea 10:12, the prophet urges his readers to "break up your fallow
   ground." Read that verse. What is fallow ground? What do you think it
   means to break up your fallow ground?

   *break up ur fallow ground; for it
   is time to seek the Lord
   till He come w rain rightousness
   upon you*

7. Hannah prays desperately about the longing and sorrow of her heart.
   After many years, God finally gives her what she has been praying for.
   What does your prayer life say about your heart? Do you pray desperately?
   Hesitantly? Gratefully? Have you given up because of disappointment?

   *Mostly gratefully, but not always
   sometimes hastily, son times
   deperately.*

8. The condition of our hearts influences how we see God. Read what a
   psalmist says to God about his heart in Psalm 19:14. What would you like
   to ask God to do regarding *your* heart? Here is a prayer that may be useful
   for you, depending on the state of your heart today:

   *Father, I've allowed the little inconveniences and the big disappointments to
   create layers of protection and distance. My disappointment and frustration
   shield me from intimacy with You. My protective shell keeps me from experiencing You fully and being known. Forgive me, Lord. Cleanse my heart, O
   God, and renew a right spirit in me (Psalm 51:10). I desire to know You and
   love You with all of my heart (Matthew 22:37).*

DAY 2

POURING OUT

Hannah's name means "grace" or "favor," but at the beginning of her story, she doesn't feel like she has God's favor. Her sadness and bitterness compel her to go before the Lord.

Coming before God with honesty and wholeheartedness releases her freedom. She pours out her misery before the Lord in prayer. Instead of allowing her misery to consume her, she approaches God with all of her disappointment.

1. Review 1 Samuel 1:10–18 and note the ways Hannah approaches the throne room of God. What are the things that characterize her honest interaction with God?

   And she was in bitterness of soul, and prayed unto the Lord and wept sore.

2. What seems to be her highest value?

   She has poured out her soul before the Lord. Strong faith.

3. How does Eli the priest perceive her?

   As drunken

4. The text says she pours out her soul, praying earnestly (verse 15). Read Psalm 42:1–5. How does this psalmist pour out his soul? What are the signs that this is not just a casual prayer?

STUDY NOTE

As I pour out my soul (Psalm 42:4). Psalm 42 is a lament—it swings back and forth from grief to hope. It takes us from remembering the past through reflecting on our present sufferings to anticipating God's vindication and presence.[9] The psalmist is not afraid to be honest with God about his feelings, yet he is also able to remind himself of what he knows is true about God.

5. Read Psalm 62. What reasons for pouring out our hearts to God does this psalmist give? Make a list of reasons, and then circle the reasons that are most significant to you.

In God is my Salvation and my glory' The rock of my Strength, and my refuge, is in God.

STUDY NOTE

For God alone (Psalm 62:1). This is a psalm of confidence. The psalmist faces calamity but shows a strong reliance on the Lord. People are untrustworthy, but God is not.[10]

6. What motivates you to pour out your soul to God? Or what keeps you from doing so? (For example, are you hindered by shortness of time, lack of faith, wrong assumptions about God, or just a self-protective spirit?)

* *Finding out someone is hurting or sad.*
* *Not sure what keeps me from Doing so. shame or guilt.*

7. Once Hannah has been honest before God and Eli, her face is no longer sad (1 Samuel 1:18). Faith gives her hope in waiting. Does honesty before God release you from oppression and lead you into hope? If so, why do you think honesty is so helpful? If not, what do you think God wants you to do in this situation?

I believe that it does. I think thats called faith.

> And we know that for those who love God all things work together for good, for those who are called according to his purpose.
>
> *Romans 8:28*

Take some time to pour out your soul to God. You can use Psalm 62 or 42 to give you ideas of what to say.

In God is my salvation and my glory, the rock of my strength.

Day 3
Persistence

> Our praying needs to be pressed and pursued with an energy that never tires, a persistency which will not be denied, and a courage that never fails.
>
> *E. M. Bounds*

Hannah continues to pray before the Lord (1 Samuel 1:12). Her process is extensive as she seeks the Lord. She has endured childlessness for years.

We sometimes tire of asking the Lord to hear our prayers, underestimating the *valuable process* of coming before Him. Approaching God is one thing, but persevering in prayer is another. Disappointment is at our heels when we tire, not seeing the results that we desire.

1. Read Luke 11:5–10. Why does the friend get out of bed and grant his neighbor's request?

STUDY NOTE

Parables. A parable is a short, realistic story that communicates a moral or spiritual lesson. Jesus taught in parables using everyday situations, usually with an unexpected twist that shocked the listener. To feel the shock, we often have to understand ancient culture. For instance, Luke 11:5 – 10 shocks the listener partly because hospitality and neighborliness were among the highest values, so only a terrible neighbor would refuse to help his friend with hospitality, even in the middle of the night.

2. Is God like this man who says, "Do not bother me" (11:7)? How, or how not? What is Jesus' point in telling this story?

3. Read Luke 18:1 – 8. Why does the judge grant the widow's request?

4. Is God like this judge? How, or how not? What is Jesus' point in telling this story?

5. Think about your persistence in prayer or lack of it. How are you picturing God when you pray?

6. When in your life have you been the most persistent in prayer, committed, pursuing God with an energy that didn't tire? What are some of the things you learned during that time? Did God show you something specific that you can remember?

7. What helps you persist in prayer now? Or what keeps you from persisting?

8. Write down one thing you want to pray for persistently. Then pour out your heart to God in prayer for that issue.

DAY 4
SURRENDER

Through surrender comes amazing strength.

Sheila Walsh

1. Though Hannah starts out bitter, after she goes to the tabernacle for years her prayers of agony move her into a place of surrender. Read 1 Samuel 1:10–28. Note the steps Hannah takes toward God, authentically releasing her pain and disappointment. Where do you see her decisive steps of surrender?

2. Imagine asking God over and over again for a child and then giving him completely to God in such a way that you would rarely see him again. What does it take to surrender a child like this? Why do you think Hannah was able to present Samuel to God as an offering?

STUDY NOTE

Vows. The laws about vows are found in Numbers 6:1–8; 30:2–16 and Deuteronomy 23:21–23. In 1 Samuel 1:11, Hannah vows to make her son a Nazirite. She will surrender him to the Lord "all the days of his life, and no razor will ever be used on his head" (NIV;

also see Numbers 6:5). Dedicating a three-year-old child to be raised by someone else is shocking to us. But in her culture, because Hannah made a binding vow to God, righteousness and blessing required her to keep it. Hannah's vow defined her son's consecration to the Lord. The Nazirite vow was normally taken for a limited period of time rather than for life.

As we read on in Scripture, we learn that Samuel grew in wisdom and obedience and became a prophet as well as a priest. He also anointed Saul and then David as the first two kings of Israel. He provided for continuity of the people's covenant with God during the transition from the rule of the judges to that of the monarchy.[11]

3. In Romans 12:1–2, Paul encourages us to present ourselves as living sacrifices to God. Paul invokes "the mercies of God"—we offer ourselves *because* of God's mercies. How has Hannah experienced God's mercies?

4. How have you experienced God's mercies?

5. What do you need to continually give to the Lord as a sacrifice of worship? This could be an attitude, a desire, a dream, an area where you suffer, something or someone you cling to. Can you present this to God? Why or why not?

6. Are there things that you have grown tired of giving over to Him? If so, why?

7. Someone once said, "I can't pray to God, I have no words; but in the morning, I drop to my knees, trusting in God's plan but unable to speak." In 1 Samuel 1:10, Hannah speaks to God. Is there an area of your life in which you need to move toward God? Can you speak to God about it? Or simply drop to your knees?

Father, I surrender the things that I hold closest to my heart. By the mercy of Christ, one bit at a time, I bring those things to You. I continue to give them over, trying to take them back and realizing I want to place them at Your feet. God, I present my life and all that is in it to You as a living and holy sacrifice. You alone are who I desire to please and worship.

DAY 5
GRATEFUL EXUBERANCE

> Just collect roses, the praise and compliments, during the day; you hold
> them, put them together in a bouquet, then at the end of the day, you
> get on your knees and say, Here, Father, these were yours all along. I just
> held them for you.
>
> *Corrie ten Boom*

In 1 Samuel 2, after Hannah receives Samuel, she expresses her deepest gratitude and praise to God. Her heart is full, and worship is on her lips, even at the moment when she is giving Samuel permanently to the Lord.

Have you ever been overwhelmed with God's blessing? And expressed it in prayer? When God overwhelms us with His presence, praise comes from our heart. But do we take the time to respond to God and praise and thank Him?

1. Read 1 Samuel 2:1–10. Make a list of the phrases Hannah uses to describe God's character and His acts.

2. Which phrase or attribute is most comforting to you as you face disappointment? Why that one?

3. Her song of joy is paralleled in a song of David in 2 Samuel 22. Which subjects repeat themselves in both?

4. Jesus' mother, Mary, was a godly young woman and most likely steeped in the Old Testament Scriptures. So she was probably very familiar with Hannah's prayer. Mary's song in Luke 1:46–55 and Hannah's prayer have many similar threads. Read Mary's song and write down the parallels you see.

Hannah (1 Samuel 2)	Mary (Luke 1)
v. 1	v. 46
v. 2	v. 49
v. 4	v. 52
v. 5	v. 53

5. How was Mary's situation like Hannah's? How was it different? (See Luke 1:26–38.)

6. Think about your own life, including disappointments and/or miracles. Write a prayer to the Lord using the guidelines of Hannah's song. Be sure to include important elements of praise, adoration, and thanksgiving.

> ## STUDY NOTE
>
> **Prayers of thanksgiving.** Notable prayers of thanksgiving, similar to Hannah's song, are offered by Miriam in Exodus 15:1–18, Moses in Deuteronomy 32:1–43, Deborah in Judges 5, and David in 2 Samuel 22.

Hannah brings her only son, Samuel, to the tabernacle at Shiloh and dedicates him to the Lord (1 Samuel 1:28). She knows that Samuel is "a rose," as Corrie ten Boom describes, part of her "bouquet." He isn't for her own benefit but for God and His glory. Her profound joy lies in presenting him back to the Lord. Jesus says in Matthew 12:34–35, "For out of the abundance of the heart the mouth speaks. The good person out of his good treasure brings forth good, and the evil person out of his evil treasure brings forth evil." Hannah's transformed heart ultimately brings forth faith, hope, and exuberant joy.

SESSION 5

FROM REGRET
TO REST

RAHAB

*For I know the plans I have for you, declares the L*ORD*, plans for welfare and not for evil, to give you a future and a hope.*

Jeremiah 29:11

REGRET CAN CONSUME A LIFE — but it doesn't have to. In this session, we'll see how God divinely reveals Himself to Rahab, a woman with a sordid past and many regrets. But God has plans for Rahab, plans to deliver her from regret into a future full of promise. He uses her life to strategically protect the nation of Israel as they attempt to conquer the first few cities in the Promised Land of Canaan. Look into her life and see the hope and future God brings to her as she responds with demonstrative faith! Through His extravagant grace, He forgives her past and redeems her into a position of honor and noteworthy faith.

WELCOME (5 minutes)

Before you watch the video, take a few minutes to share the following:

> Some people almost never look back and feel regret. Others are consumed by regret for what has happened in the past. On a scale of 0 to 5, where 0 = never and 5 = intensely and often, how much is regret a part of your life?

```
|———————————+———————————+———————————+———————————|
1           2           3           4           5
```

VIDEO: FROM REGRET TO REST (21 minutes)

Play the video segment for Session 5. As you watch, use the outline provided to follow along or to take notes on anything that stands out to you.

NOTES

Regret is a small word. At times it reflects a decision as lightweight as backing out of dinner plans. But sometimes regret can consume your life.

No matter how many wrong choices we make, God is still in control and watching over us.

Regret dissolves as we enter into the greatness of God's plan.

Rahab was ready to step *out* of regret and *into* relationship with God.

"In him you also, when you heard the word of truth, the gospel of your salvation, and believed in him, were sealed with the promised Holy Spirit, who is the guarantee of our inheritance until we acquire possession of it, to the praise of his glory" (Ephesians 1:13 – 14).

Rahab was marked with faith that guaranteed the security of her family.

Her life was no longer defined by where she had walked but by her new life in God and His plans.

The shedding of Christ's blood saves us.

Don't allow regret for what you have done to rob you of the joy of who you are.

Practical steps to letting go:

1. Take your deepest regrets to the cross.
2. Be honest and own your regret.
3. Make amends where possible.
4. Grieve your losses.
5. Forgive.

GROUP DISCUSSION

VIDEO DEBRIEF (5 minutes)

> *If your group meets for two hours,*
> *allow 10 minutes for this discussion.*

1. What was one insight from the video that gave you encouragement or a new way to look at things?

FROM REGRET TO FAITH (10 minutes)

> *If your group meets for two hours,*
> *allow 15 minutes for this discussion.*

2. Read aloud Joshua 2:1 – 11. What happens in Rahab's heart between verses 1 and 11?

3. How does Rahab demonstrate that she has stopped regretting her past and is now focused on faith in God?

4. Checkmark which one of the following parts of that process is most challenging for you to accept and respond to. Then if you feel comfortable doing so, share with your group the challenge you face.

❑ **Ceasing to regret my past.** I have issues in my life that rob me of believing that God has a plan for my life and redeems my regrets.

❑ **Having faith in God.** I have trouble believing that God is who the Bible says He is and that His qualities are greater than my regrets.

❑ **Receiving His grace.** I have been unable to receive His grace and mercy that are offered to me on the cross.

❑ **Acting in faith.** I am scared to step out in faith and take a risk based on God's promises to me.

5. Despite her family history and the pagan beliefs of Jericho, Rahab *believed* in the God of Israel—and this changed everything. Likewise, believing God is foundational to our confidence as we let go of regret. What qualities of God do you have difficulty believing? Take a moment on your own to check the qualities of God you struggle with, and then share with your group which ones you checked.

(The corresponding verses are provided for you to look up on your own after the group meeting. Or if your group meets for two hours, see the optional exercise in the shaded box below.)

❑ Faithful (1 Corinthians 1:9)   ❑ Loving (Psalm 86:15)
❑ Provider (Psalm 54:4)   ❑ Wise (Romans 11:33)
❑ Compassionate (Psalm 103:8)   ❑ Trustworthy (Psalm 9:10)
❑ Powerful (Jeremiah 10:12)   ❑ Strong (Jeremiah 16:19)
❑ Protector (Psalm 18:2)   ❑ Redeemer (Isaiah 49:7)

OPTIONAL GROUP DISCUSSION *(15 minutes)*

BELIEVING GOD

- Look at your answers to question 5. What do you think hinders you from believing that God has those qualities?
- Look up some of the verses listed in question 5. How do those verses affect you? How do or don't they help you believe God has these qualities?

HOPE AND FORGIVENESS (10 minutes)

> *If your group meets for two hours,*
> *allow 25 minutes for this discussion.*

6. Read Jeremiah 29:11. Have you ever made a choice you regret, but God still showed His future and hope for you? If so, share that experience with the group.

STUDY NOTE

A future and a hope (Jeremiah 29:11). Jeremiah encourages God's people by promising them a future: seventy years after the beginning of their exile, He will restore them to their land (29:10). It's hard for them to trust, knowing that this won't take place until their grandchildren's time. But God's timing is always perfect no matter how things may appear.

7. Have you experienced forgiveness from the shame and guilt of past decisions and choices? If so, tell one way forgiveness affects the way you live
now or one reason you know you've been forgiven.

STUDY NOTE

Hope. The Hebrew word for "hope," *tiqwah*, means a cord. Figura-
tively, it means to look for or wait. It is directly tied to God's promises; to security in the ultimate destination of God's promises, not
our desires or plans; and to security in the final destination of God's
greater story. *Tiqwah* is used in Joshua 2 to refer to Rahab's cord.
(See also Joshua 2:18, 21 and Genesis 49:18).

8. Briefly describe a current choice or situation where you are having difficulty believing or seeing the hope in God's plans.

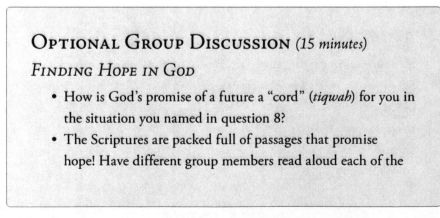

OPTIONAL GROUP DISCUSSION (15 *minutes*)
FINDING HOPE IN GOD

- How is God's promise of a future a "cord" (*tiqwah*) for you in
  the situation you named in question 8?
- The Scriptures are packed full of passages that promise
  hope! Have different group members read aloud each of the

passages below. How does each promise hope and strength? Does one of them stand out as especially helpful to you? If so, tell why.

Psalm 3:3–4	Zephaniah 3:17
Romans 5:2–5	Romans 15:13
2 Corinthians 4:16–18	1 Peter 1:3

- Regret diminishes as we trust God's plans. Our challenge is to see God's plans not just as different from our own—confusing and frustrating—but as greater than our own. Read aloud Isaiah 55:8–9. Do you sometimes find it hard to believe that God's plans are trustworthy? If so, does Isaiah 55:8–9 help to explain why, or do you have other reasons for mistrusting God's plans?

ACTIVE FAITH (10 minutes)

If your group meets for two hours, take 15 minutes for this section.

9. Take a moment on your own to meditate on Jeremiah 29:11. Insert your name in the blanks below.

For I know the plans I have for _____, declares the LORD, plans for welfare and not for evil, to give you _____ a future and a hope.

10. Recall from question 8 the area of your life where you question God's plan. Briefly remind the group what that area is. Take particular note of what the person on your right shares, because you're going to pray for her.

Now, take the words of Jeremiah 29:11, and with the authority of the truth, pray for life over each member in the group. Pray for the person on your right, inserting her name in the prayer below and adding any requests that come to you. May God's Word become alive and produce a future and a hope for each person sitting in your group.

Dear God, I know the plans you have for _____, the plans You declare, plans for welfare and not for evil, to give _____ a future and a hope. We thank You, God, that we can trust You implicitly and know You delight in building _____'s life with great intention no matter what she has faced. Thank You for the hope You provide for _____. Thank You for the promise. Thank You for Your individual and wonderful plan. In Jesus' name and the hope that comes in Him, Amen.

Her life was no longer defined by where she had walked but her new life in God and His plans.

Sheila Walsh

PERSONAL STUDIES

DAY 1
STRONG AND COURAGEOUS

Regret dissolves as we enter into the greatness of God's plan.
Sheila Walsh

Before we get more acquainted with Rahab's story, let's establish the historical background that led the spies to enter her house.

By the end of the book of Deuteronomy, the Israelites have wandered in the wilderness for forty years after their exodus from Egypt. Up until this point, Joshua has been second-in-command to Moses. But now, as Moses' life nears its end, he calls Joshua to lead the Israelites into the Promised Land. This is the land God promised to Israel centuries earlier (Genesis 15:13–21). At last it's all coming true.

1. Read Deuteronomy 31:1–8. What does God (through Moses) promise He will do for the Israelites and Joshua?

   What does God tell the Israelites to do?

   What does He tell Joshua to do?

The reason the Lord isn't letting Moses lead the people into Canaan is that he committed a serious sin (Numbers 20:2–13). But Moses has overcome regret by seeing that God's plan is greater than his own. Joshua will lead the people instead.

(A beautiful picture of the grace of God can be seen in Matthew 17:1–3. Here Christ is seen by his three closest friends, transfigured and standing on a mountain in the Promised Land with Moses and Elijah. Moses makes it after all!)

As the Israelites enter the Promised Land, they come upon Jericho, one of the fortified cities just inside the border. Jericho is most likely well prepared for a siege, with a stream inside the city walls and a harvest just gathered.

God tells Joshua, "I will be with you. I will not leave you or forsake you" (Joshua 1:5). This is a wonderful promise as we walk out of regret and into trusting God and His promises. In the Old Testament, hope and trust are essentially synonymous. To hope means to trust. Often our fear keeps us from living in the reality of God's promises.

A few verses later, God connects His presence with obedience. Our lack of obedience limits God's abundant plan for our lives.

> Only be strong and very courageous, being careful to do according to all the law that Moses my servant commanded you. Do not turn from it to the right hand or to the left, that you may have good success wherever you go. This Book of the Law shall not depart from your mouth, but you shall meditate on it day and night, so that you may be careful to do according to all that is written in it. For then you will make your way prosperous, and then you will have good success. (Joshua 1:7–8)

2. Have you suffered any consequences of not fully obeying God? If so, do you believe God wants to give you another chance, or do you believe it's all over for you? Why?

Study Note

Meditate. In Hebrew, *hagah*, to murmur or to ponder. This means more than to simply think upon. It means to study, talk about, utter. The Hebrews will recall God's goodness and faithfulness by retelling the ancient stories. This is meditation.

3. Has God challenged you to let go of regret and walk somewhere new, but you have lacked the courage to walk in faith? If so, what would walking in faith look like? What is God asking of you?

4. What role has fear played in thwarting God's plans for you? Where would you not go because of fear?

5. What are you afraid of now?

6. Read Joshua 1:6–9. How does this passage give you confidence? (Or if it doesn't, explain why not.)

It's crucial for us to understand that when God makes His promises to us, when He leads us from regret into relationship and faith, He will establish our territory and He will not fail or leave us. Even if we feel regret, when we follow God and walk in obedience, we can trust His plans and His continual presence and faithfulness.

7. Read Psalm 100:5. What does it say about God's faithfulness?

8. List some areas of your life where you have seen God's faithfulness. (Examples: health, marriage, friendships, career, finances, emotional healing.)

Meditate, ponder, and speak of God's faithfulness in these areas of your life as God instructs us to do in Joshua 1:8–9.

9. God tells Joshua, "The LORD your God is with you wherever you go" (1:9). Jesus tells His disciples the same thing in Matthew 28:20. Read Matthew 28:16–20. What do you think is significant about Jesus repeating this promise?

10. As you seek to walk in faith, you will face obstacles or battles. Consider the list below or add your own. After establishing your obstacles, find a promise of God that will help you overcome that obstacle. Take some time to read the verses on the right.

Your Obstacle/Battle	God's Promise
Fear	Isaiah 41:10
Forgiveness	Isaiah 1:18
Timidity	2 Timothy 1:7
Insecurity	Deuteronomy 33:12
Shame	Psalm 40:11–12
Other:	
Other:	

As you seek to be strong and courageous in obeying God today, pray for His help.

Lord, You go before me. You conquer and fulfill Your plans through Your great and mighty hand. I claim courage and strength because You are with me. I do not turn to the right or left, Lord, but walk in faithfulness to You, trusting in You. I trust in Your Word day and night, asking You for guidance as I lead, walk, stumble, and conquer. In Jesus' name, Amen.

Day 2
Beyond Regret

With the authority of God's Word and the undergirding of strength and courage, Joshua is preparing to conquer Jericho and lead the Israelites into Canaan. He decides to send spies into Jericho to gather intelligence.

> And Joshua the son of Nun sent two men secretly from Shittim as spies, saying, "Go, view the land, especially Jericho." And they went and came into the house of a prostitute whose name was Rahab and lodged there. (Joshua 2:1)

Surprise, surprise. This is a huge moment for Joshua, the culmination of a promise that has been transpiring for over forty years, and who does God drop into the picture as a heroine? Rahab the prostitute! God says His ways

Study Note

Rahab the prostitute. Before the encounter with the spies, Rahab's life was most likely full of regret. Rahab's name means "wide" or "broad." It also means "insolence." The Amorite people are idolatrous and live insolent lives, far from God. A harlot is an outcast—alienated and lonely. Society shuns her. Men use her for one purpose and one purpose only.

She has no spiritual or moral value—no Sabbath, no teachings, no teacher. Her life is a prime example of the vile corruption of Canaan. Israel is God's chosen people, and Canaan is His rejected people because of their godless abandonment to sin and their rejection of the true God. They worship sex and participate in orgies.

Some have suggested that the Hebrew word translated "prostitute" means innkeeper. Her home was situated by the wall, and possibly at the entrance.

are not our ways. How would we ever suspect that out of all the people God could use to help conquer Jericho, it would be a harlot! The providence of God directed the spies to her house. Never underestimate how God can use you in His greater story!

Think about regret. Without Christ, regret punishes with no end in sight. This is surely true for Rahab, who lives with the daily reality of life as a prostitute, but isn't it true for all of us? We make decisions that set our course, decisions we cannot take back, decisions that leave punishment. Our reality is dictated by our past and present decisions.

Our gracious and loving God has a different idea about regret. He has a different idea about second chances. As 2 Chronicles 16:9 says, "For the eyes of the LORD run to and fro throughout the whole earth, to give strong support to those whose heart is blameless toward him."

1. Look up the following passages and write down your observations about how God looks at second chances.

   Job 33:26–30

   Psalm 30:2–3

   Psalm 130:3–8

   Isaiah 43:25

In the perverse city of Jericho, God notices one woman who has faith in what she has heard about the God of Israel (2:11). He sends the spies to this *one* woman and offers grace and forgiveness to *one* who believes what she has heard. God chooses Rahab to help navigate the success of the Israelites in Jericho. God sees Rahab as valuable, redeemable, significant. Rahab acts on what she knows about God, overcomes her past, and embraces God by faith.

Think about your own life. Are you a person who needs to see more of God's heart and His desire to redeem your life and behavior?

2. Name some of your decisions that you have considered unredeemable.

3. In what ways do you live with the consequences of regret that disable you from the loving and redemptive plans of the Father?

4. Sometimes regret comes not just from the choices we have made but from circumstances beyond our control—maybe times when we have been a victim. Do you look at your past with regret? Which, if any, of these areas have left "punishment" in your life?

    ❑ Infidelity   ❑ Addiction
    ❑ Family history   ❑ Blame
    ❑ Abuse or rape   ❑ Other: _____
    ❑ Marriage

5. What are some of the negative consequences you have suffered as a result of these circumstances?

In the shadow of my hurt, forgiveness feels like a decision to reward my enemy. But in the shadow of the cross, forgiveness is merely a gift from one undeserving soul to another.

Andy Stanley

6. Are you willing to let go of regret and allow God to give you "strong support" as promised in 2 Chronicles 16:9, as you bring your broken heart before Him? If so, then write a prayer in which you offer your regret and your broken heart to God. Write out your forgiveness toward those who have harmed you (including yourself). Ask for God's strong support.

   Or if you don't feel ready to forgive, write whatever prayer is true for you right now.

The greatness of our regret or sin does not hinder the abundance of grace that God extends to one with a repentant heart. As we repent and bring our regret and sin before God, He removes them and shows compassion.

7. Read Psalm 103:11–12. Draw a picture that shows the way the psalmist describes where your sin is compared to where you are, and where God's love for you is.

8. Read 2 Corinthians 7:10 and Philippians 3:13–15 and list some action steps to abandon regret.

9. What might one of these action steps look like in your situation?

> There is more to life than meets the eye. For that's what faith is. Faith is trusting what the eye can't see. Eyes see the prowling lion. Faith sees Daniel's angel. Eyes see storms. Faith sees Noah's rainbow. Eyes see giants. Faith sees Canaan.
>
> *Max Lucado*

10. As you acknowledge your history, regrets, or sin, how can you invite God to take your life and gently infuse it with grace and redemption? Take some time to write about letting God into your places of regret. Be honest with Him, releasing your regret and allowing God's truth to transform you.

Father, I am so thankful for Your endless love and compassion. I confess my poor decisions, my doubt, and the parts of life that I regret. I trust You to remove these things from Your sight as far as the east is from the west. Your healing grace is sufficient for me. Your power is made perfect in my weakness. Your ways are high above all that I can ever imagine. You see me, Lord, wherever I am and seek me out, desiring to strengthen, renew, and redeem. Thank You, Lord. In Jesus' name, Amen.

DAY 3
DECLARING FAITH

Today we will look at Rahab's proclamation of faith. Before her verbal proclamation, she takes a big risk by taking the spies into her home and hiding them from the king.

1. Read Joshua 2:2–7. What does the king ask of Rahab?

How does she respond? What does she say and do?

How do her words and actions require faith?

STUDY NOTE

Flax. Flax had long been grown in Egypt and Palestine as a fiber for clothing, cords, and bands. It was customary to use rooftops for drying grain or stalks of flax, where they could be piled several feet high. Besides working as a harlot, Rahab apparently worked with flax. She could have turned to her flax business to free herself from prostitution. She might then have felt no need of God's redemption. But her hunger was deeper than a need for a career change; she needed a life transformation that would take her from despair to hope.

2. As soon as the pursuers are gone, Rahab confesses her faith to the spies. Read Joshua 2:8 – 11. How would you put into your own words what she believes about God?

Why does Rahab recall two particular events in Israel's history — the incident at the Red Sea and the confrontation with the Amorite kings? As you learn about these two events, reflect on three things: God's *power*, God's *presence*, and God's *permanence*.

3. Read Exodus 14:21 – 31. What observations can you make about God? What does He do?

4. How might God's power, presence, and permanence have struck Rahab after hearing this?

5. Now read about Sihon and Og in Numbers 21:21 – 35. How does this incident reveal God's power, presence, and permanence to Rahab?

Many in the fortified cities of Canaan had heard of these events:

Rise up, set out on your journey and go over the Valley of the Arnon.
Behold, I have given into your hand Sihon the Amorite, king of Heshbon,
and his land. Begin to take possession, and contend with him in battle.
This day I will begin to put the dread and fear of you on the peoples who
are under the whole heaven, who shall hear the report of you and shall
tremble and be in anguish because of you. (Deuteronomy 2:24 – 25)

Jericho waited in fear. They had heard about the victories; they knew
God had promised Israel the possession of the land; and yet they chose not
to believe. We all have a choice.

6. Reflect on the God who parted the Red Sea, the God who revealed Himself to Rahab. What might this God be calling you to do because of *His*
   greatness?

7. Like Rahab, what do you need to believe, contrary to your history, in
   order to rest in God's truths and walk in His plans?

8. Take some time to praise God and acknowledge your faith in Him. Use a
   colored pen or marker to underline all of the things in the following verses
   that are true about God. Truth can be an anchor for our faith.

Praise the LORD!
Praise the LORD, O my soul!
I will praise the LORD as long as I live;
     I will sing praises to my God while I have my being.
Put not your trust in princes,
     in a son of man, in whom there is no salvation. (*cont.*)

When his breath departs, he returns to the earth;
    on that very day his plans perish.
Blessed is he whose help is the God of Jacob,
    whose hope is in the LORD his God,
who made heaven and earth,
    the sea, and all that is in them,
who keeps faith forever;
    who executes justice for the oppressed,
    who gives food to the hungry.
The LORD sets the prisoners free;
    the LORD opens the eyes of the blind.
The LORD lifts up those who are bowed down;
    the LORD loves the righteous.
The LORD watches over the sojourners;
    he upholds the widow and the fatherless,
    but the way of the wicked he brings to ruin.
The LORD will reign forever,
    your God, O Zion, to all generations.
Praise the LORD!

Psalm 146

DAY 4
FAITH IN ACTION

Faith is demonstrated through our desire to live it out. James 2:26 states that "faith apart from works is dead." Rahab was justified by the faith she demonstrated through her works: hiding the spies, risking the king's punishment, and asking for her family's protection.

1. Read James 2:14–26. Why does James think faith without works is dead?

> ## STUDY NOTE
>
> **Go in peace (James 2:16).** This was a familiar Jewish blessing, but it was expected that mercy would accompany the blessing. "Be warmed" speaks to how cold the homeless could become in winter in a high-elevation city like Jerusalem. Words alone without the heart of Christ are faithless.

2. Think of Rahab as an example. What would "faith" amount to in her case if she believed what she said in Joshua 2:8–11, but then turned the spies over to the king of Jericho?

3. What does James mean in James 2:25 when he says Rahab was justified by her works? Does he mean that her faith was irrelevant?

In Rahab we see the perfect example of a budding faith that prompted her to action. The word for "justify" in James 2:25 is *dikaioo*, which speaks to an act of God bringing sinners into relationship with Him.

4. How does your own life display—or not display—this combination of faith and works? Do you tend to believe in God but not express your belief through action? Or do you do a lot but not really believe? Or does your faith often lead to actions?

5. Read Joshua 2:12–21. Rahab's faith affected her whole family. What impact does your faith have on your family and neighbors?

6. Do your regrets and fears hinder your influence? If so, how?

7. Draw a simple family tree that shows your potential influence of faith and prayer for your family.

The cord of scarlet thread tied in the window (Joshua 2:21) marked Rahab's home as a house of faith and secured her family. The red resembled the blood of the Passover lamb that protected the Israelites when the Lord struck down the firstborn of Egypt (Exodus 12:13, 22–23). The early church viewed the scarlet cord as a symbol of Christ's atonement.

Take a moment to pray for God to rescue each person in your family as He rescued each member of Rahab's family. Pray also for yourself:

> *God, You alone guarantee an inheritance beyond my wildest dreams. I act in faith, building life from Your foundation, rather than my regret, trusting and walking one step at a time. I hang my cord, the blood of Christ, symbolizing the forgiveness, the protection, and the freedom I have because of You. My faith in You and Your blood provides all the protection and power to be saved from my regret and its consequences. I also ask You to cover each member of my family with this same protection. Because of Jesus and His blood, Amen.*

Rahab was marked in the faith that guaranteed the security of her family.

Sheila Walsh

DAY 5
REFLECTING BACK

Look back at your notes from the video and group discussion, and at your personal study on Days 1 through 4. Prayerfully respond to these questions.

1. What have been the one or two main things you believe God has been trying to say to you?

2. Has what you've learned affected your relationship with God or other people in any way? If so, how?

Don't allow regret for what you have done to rob you of the joy of who you are.

Sheila Walsh

3. Have you taken any action as a result of what God is saying? If so, what did you do? (Small steps count.)

4. Is there anything else you believe God wants you to do? If so, what?

5. What help will you need from God? From others?

Pray as you close:

Heavenly Father, thank You for forgiving me and cleansing me from all my regret through the blood of Christ. I let down the scarlet rope with faith and confidence in the blood of Christ that redeems my life. I look forward to Your greater plans — the things You planned for my life long ago. I have faith and desire to take action and possession, God, of all that You desire for me. I desire to please You, God, and walk in places that I can't see yet but believe You can take me. I rest in the confidence of Your character and truth. Because of Jesus, Amen.

Never be afraid to trust an unknown future to a known God.

Corrie ten Boom

FROM INSECURITY
TO CONFIDENCE

RUTH

Trust in the LORD with all your heart, and do not lean on your own understanding. In all your ways acknowledge him, and he will make straight your paths.

Proverbs 3:5–6

WE LIVE IN AN INSECURE WORLD. A gunman walks into a suburban school and shoots children. Bombs explode at a marathon. A medical test reveals a heartbreaking illness. A corporation lays off hundreds of workers. No matter how we try to control our surroundings, we can't guarantee security for ourselves or our loved ones.

What can we do about that? We can live with crippling anxiety. We can wall ourselves off to create the illusion of security. Or we can throw ourselves into the arms of a good God. In this session, we'll look at the story of a young woman who takes that last option. Ruth is a widow, an immigrant with no money. She bets her life on the goodness of the God of Israel, and by persistently taking action based on trust, she becomes a player in a story that changes the world.

WELCOME (5 minutes)

As we set the stage for the story of Ruth, take a few minutes to share the following:

What areas of your life increase your feelings of insecurity?

VIDEO: FROM INSECURITY TO CONFIDENCE (21 minutes)

Play the video segment for Session 6. As you watch, use the outline provided to follow along or to take notes on anything that stands out to you.

NOTES

Insecure means "not safe; not confident of security."

The Moabites were a cursed people because of their perverse origin and pagan beliefs (Genesis 19, Deuteronomy 23).

Do you ever ask questions of God that you never thought you would ask?

Ruth, who became the great-grandmother of David and an ancestress of Jesus, began her journey as a pagan, outside of the family of Jehovah and part of a cursed people.

Ruth's life foreshadows God's plan of redemption through grace and conformity to the will of God through faith, rather than through blood and birth.

God's greatest blessings come as we take risks.

God can take what might feel like your lost life and bring meaning and blessing to you in the most surprising ways.

God redeems our past.

The most secure place in life is with God Himself.

> The further we travel on this pathway to glory the more glorious it becomes, because we are given to understand that every glad surrender of self . . . is merely a little death, like the tree's "loss" of the dead leaf, in order that a fresh new one may, in God's time, take its place.
>
> *Elisabeth Elliot*

GROUP DISCUSSION

VIDEO DEBRIEF (5 *minutes*)

> *If your group meets for two hours,*
> *allow 10 minutes for this discussion.*

1. What was most meaningful to you in Sheila's teaching on Naomi and Ruth? What did you learn, or what did you identify with?

INSECURITY *(10 minutes)*

> *If your group meets for two hours,*
> *allow 20 minutes for this discussion.*

2. How would you define the two words below?

Insecurity

Humility

Be careful not to mistake insecurity and inadequacy for humility! Humility has nothing to do with the insecure and inadequate! Just like arrogance has nothing to do with greatness!

C. JoyBell C.

3. Read the first chapter of Ruth. What are some of the circumstances that cause Ruth and Naomi to experience insecurity?

STUDY NOTES

In the days when the judges ruled (Ruth 1:1). The time of the judges was a time of violence, immorality, and political chaos. During one eighteen-year period, the Moabites invaded Israel and forced the people to pay annual tribute (Judges 3:12–30). The Israelites never forgot that incident nor Moab's earlier hostility in Moses' day (Deuteronomy 23:3–5). Israel's prophets later denounced the Moabites for their oppression, pride, and arrogance (Isaiah 15–16; Jeremiah 48).

Moabite (1:4). Ruth was a Moabite. Marriage to a Moabite woman was not forbidden, but no Moabite — or his descendants to the tenth generation — was allowed to "enter the assembly of the LORD" (Deuteronomy 23:3). The Israelites almost certainly viewed Moabite immigrants with contempt.

4. How reasonable would it be to feel insecure in Naomi's situation? What about in Ruth's situation? Why?

OPTIONAL GROUP DISCUSSION (15 *minutes*)

DERAILED

- How does Naomi respond to her insecure situation?
- Insecurity rises up in all of us. Share about a time when you felt insecure. What circumstances led you to feel that way?

TRUSTING (10 MINUTES)

> *If your group meets for two hours,*
> *allow 20 minutes for this discussion.*

If I obey Jesus Christ in the seemingly random circumstances of life, they become pinholes through which I see the face of God.

Oswald Chambers

5. Naomi and Ruth are living in tough times. Moral degradation, famine, and oppression are at a peak. Women without husbands are vulnerable. Yet amid these harsh circumstances, as demonstrated again and again throughout Scripture, God has a redemptive plan. What seems to be discouraging and confusing often leads to some of God's greatest work! Read Proverbs 3:5 – 6, where we find tremendous encouragement for those times when we face circumstances that make us question God and His plans. In your own words, what does it mean to "trust"?

STUDY NOTE

Trust. The Hebrew word is *batah*: to rely on someone else for security. The proverb invites us to rely on the Lord to keep us safe, to have confidence in Him and not in our own understanding.

6. In the first chapter of Ruth, how does Ruth do what Proverbs 3:5–6 says? What decisions does she make? What actions? How do her actions show reliance on the Lord rather than her own understanding?

OPTIONAL GROUP DISCUSSION (25 *minutes*)

ALL YOUR HEART

- What reasons for trusting God do Psalm 4; Psalm 56:11; and 2 Corinthians 1:8–10 give?
- Like many of us, Naomi is overcome by her situation. She questions God. Her own understanding of reality drives her to despair. Read Ruth 1:16–22, and compare Naomi's perspective with Ruth's. What are the differences between them?
- How does Ruth demonstrate trust in God?
- One of the key words in Proverbs 3:5 is *all*. It is used twice—once concerning your heart and once concerning your behavior. God desires us to trust with a whole heart, not a divided heart. Our human nature leans toward self-dependence. Proverbs implies that our own understanding is in direct conflict with God's way and plans. Have you ever seen a divided heart complicate your own trust in God's plans? How?
- Do you see any remnant of division in Ruth's heart? Which verses in Ruth 1 verify your conclusion?
- Why do you think it is important to trust in the Lord with *all* of your heart?

ACTIVE TRUST (10 minutes)

7. Think about a situation in your life that brings you insecurity and requires trust. Take five minutes on your own to answer the following questions:

   • What is your understanding of the situation? What are the details or circumstances that surround you?

   • Does your understanding fit or conflict with the confidence that God may want to give you through this? If it conflicts, give a specific example of how.

   If there is time, tell the group what you learned from your reflection.

8. Read Psalm 37:5. The Hebrew word for "commit" is *galal*, literally, "to roll up." The psalmist invites you to "roll up" your way onto the Lord. How can you give your insecurity to God, rolling it upon Him, instead of holding it yourself?

Ruth was able to commit her way to the Lord and trust. Pray together, committing to the Lord the situation you identified in question 7.

Father, we commit our lives to You. Our circumstances create insecurity and doubt. We trust in You, and we do not lean on our own vision of what is happening around us now or in the days ahead. We "roll" our worry and life onto You, God, asking that as we trust, You will slowly reveal Your ways to us. In Jesus' name, Amen.

PERSONAL STUDIES

DAY 1
INSECURITY

The story of Ruth is set in a time of religious and moral degeneracy, foreign oppression, and disunity among the tribes of Israel. Joshua is dead, and the Israelites have failed to fully take possession of Canaan. They are led by a series of "judges" (Hebrew: *shoftim*), who are primarily war leaders rather than lawmakers.

Only two biblical books are named after women: Ruth and Esther. Ruth is a Moabite—not an Israelite, not a Jew. God cursed Moab because Moab rejected Him in every way. This curse is in full force as the book of Ruth begins. Ruth loses her husband and becomes an impoverished immigrant from a land God has cursed. Yet she places her faith in God, and He bestows on her the honor of becoming the great-grandmother of King David and an ancestress of Jesus (Matthew 1:1, 5).

1. In your group discussion, you saw the insecure situation Ruth faced. Review Ruth 1 and list the challenges she confronted.

2. Scripture tells of many great followers of God who started out lacking, insecure, in places where it was hard to see God's redemptive work in their lives. Faith in God consistently led them into confidence and stature. One

of those faithful people is David, Ruth's great-grandson. Read 1 Samuel 17. In verses 1–31, what reasons do you see for David to be insecure?

3. How does the text describe the way David found security in God as he moved forward? What specific statements and actions reflect his attitude toward God?

4. If you didn't know the end of the story, what would go through your mind if you heard someone talking and acting the way David did?

5. What results did David see as he walked in the confidence of the Lord?

6. We can be grateful if we never face the level of insecurity Ruth had to deal with as a penniless immigrant from a hated country. Which of the following issues are areas of insecurity for you? (At the end of the checklist, add any other issues that cause you insecurity.)

❑ Appearance   ❑ Starting over
❑ Skills   ❑ Comparison
❑ Pleasing people   ❑ Status
❑ Finances   ❑ Change
❑ Living situation   ❑ Other (name it):
❑ Relationships
❑ Accomplishments   _____
❑ Image   ❑ Other (name it):
❑ Loss
❑ New places   _____
                         ❑ Other (name it):

                         _____

7. Read 2 Corinthians 12:7 – 10. What does Paul say about insecurity in light of the work of Christ in our lives?

8. In the chart below, write down up to three areas you feel insecure about on the left. If you see a hint of God's plan for you, write those things on the right.

Insecure Area	God's Plans

9. With the same areas of insecurity in mind, what steps of faith or Scriptures might provide confidence as you walk into God's plans? (Some passages to consider are Psalm 52:8–9; Psalm 56:3–4; Psalm 61:1–4; Psalm 63:1–8; Proverbs 3:5–6; and Philippians 1:25–26.)

Insecure Area	Steps of Faith/Scriptures
Example: Upcoming move to a new city	Pray for new friends Pray for a new church home Get a group of current friends together to pray Meditate on Proverbs 3:5–6

Offer your areas of insecurity to God in prayer. If the following prayer fits where you are right now, use it (filling in the blanks) or adapt it.

God, I bring my insecurity and affliction before You. I feel like Naomi — my identity is determined by my fear — and yet I walk in the confidence of Your plans. I bring my _____ and _____. I do not lean on my own understanding of these things, but walk in faith and trust, leaning into the confidence I have in You. You will be my confidence and keep my feet from being snared. In Jesus' name, Amen.

DAY 2
HUMILITY

> Humility belongs to a different family than insecurity.
>
> *Sheila Walsh*

Today we are going to look further into the story of Ruth and how her humility led her into the purposes of God. Her process of humility and "emptying" began with the death of her husband (Ruth 1:3). It didn't stop there.

1. Read Ruth chapters 2 and 3 and note below with verse references all the times you observe Ruth demonstrating an attitude of humility.

STUDY NOTE

Gleaning (Ruth 2:17–23; Leviticus 19:9–10). To glean is to collect leftovers from the edges of a field after it has been harvested. The law of Moses gave the poor, widows, and orphans the right to glean landowners' fields. This was a form of care or welfare.

---

2. Christ is our highest model of humility. Read Philippians 2:5–11. From this passage, list the ways Jesus demonstrated humility. (You may find as many as seven ways. See the example below.)

    v. 6 *He did not regard equality with God a thing to be grasped.*
    v. 7

v. 7

v. 7

v. 8

v. 8

v. 8

STUDY NOTE

Emptied himself (Philippians 2:7). The Greek verb *kenoo* means "to empty." It gives us the noun *kenosis*, which refers to Jesus' act of emptying Himself and taking the form of a bond servant. Many Christians over the centuries have meditated on what it meant for Christ to empty Himself of His rights as the divine Son of God, to add limitations to Himself by becoming a mortal man who experienced hunger, weariness, pain, and even death.

3. God exalted Jesus through His humility. Look again at Philippians 2:9–11 and identify the various ways God exalted Jesus.

v. 9 *God highly exalted Him.*
v. 9

v. 10

v. 10

v. 10

v. 10

v. 11

4. What is the connection between Jesus' humility and His exaltation? Who did the humbling? Who did the exalting?

5. How are Jesus' humility and Ruth's humility different from feelings of worthlessness? Does Ruth act like she feels worthless? What do you see in the Bible text?

A lack of humility stems from pride—the desire to be in control; the belief that we are more important, more gifted, or have greater potential than others. Ironically, feelings of worthlessness and insecurity are also rooted in pride: we feel worthless when we fail to achieve the impossible standard we or others set for us. Self-exaltation and self-contempt are twin sisters, the daughters of pride.

6. How do you respond to the obstacles and trials in your life? Do you respond with humility? Do you take the reins and try to power through the obstacles? Do you quickly feel helpless and give up?

7. Does a lack of humility keep you from growing in the confidence and plans that God may have for you? If so, how?

Ask God where you need to humble yourself in order to align yourself with His plans. Spend some time bringing those areas before the Lord and asking Him to deepen your humility as you walk with Him.

> Humility is that overwhelming understanding that the awesome God of the universe, Lord of all creation, loves us and invites us to join in with His redemptive plan for this fallen world.
>
> *Sheila Walsh*

DAY 3
VIRTUE

Apart from the Proverbs 31 wife, Ruth is the only woman in the Bible specifically called virtuous (Ruth 3:11). The words *virtuous* and *virtue* (Hebrew: *chayil* and related forms) are used over 200 times in the Hebrew Bible. *Chayil* means wealth, virtue, valor, strength, integrity, noble character. Merriam-Webster defines *virtuous* as "morally excellent." Virtue includes all areas of life, not just sexuality.

This woman, not even a Jew, is the one called a "virtuous woman." Once again, God plucks out the most unlikely candidate to set in a prominent place. Do you feel like your story is the exception to God's ability to redeem a broken life and usher you into a greater plan? Do you feel like His greater plans are for everyone except you?

Ruth isn't a Jew; she stands in complete chaos, and yet God in His redemptive plan provides for her and sends her a redeemer. In this process, her purity of heart matters.

1. Ruth begins by expressing faith in Naomi's God. How does she do this (1:16–17)?

2. With her faith in God established, she steps forward with purity of heart. Where do you see her acting with virtue and purity of heart in Ruth 2:1–3:18?

3. What is Ruth risking as she devotes herself to Naomi, both supporting her and following her plans?

4. What does Ruth sacrifice in pursuing Boaz rather than other men?

5. What are the results of her virtue? How does it affect her relationship with Naomi? With Boaz? With others in Bethlehem? (Consider Ruth 2:1 – 4:22.)

6. How does purity of heart affect one's life and future? What do the verses below say about this?

    Psalm 24:4 – 5

    Proverbs 22:11

    Matthew 5:8

7. In what way is God asking you to step forward in virtue?

8. Read the following three verses. How does Ruth embody each of these aspects of a virtuous woman's experience?

    Proverbs 31:10

    Proverbs 31:23

Proverbs 31:31

9. Is there a place in your life where God is leading you, and your heart's impurity is limiting God's blessings? If so, what is that place?

Spend some time today asking God to purify your heart. Meditate on Psalms 19:14; 51:10, 17.

DAY 4

REDEMPTION

Ruth's story is a picture of the redemption Christ offers. The Hebrew word group for "redeem/redeemer/redemption" occurs twenty-three times in the book. Ruth embraces Naomi's God (1:16), and Boaz then offers her protection and life (2:8–12). Naomi too is redeemed.

Like a lost sinner, Ruth can do nothing to save herself. She puts herself in a position to trust God's faithfulness. He in turn brings her confidence and grace through the care of Naomi and the grace of Boaz.

1. Read Ruth 2:8–17. How does Ruth respond to Boaz's grace?

2. How does Ruth request that he redeem her (3:9)?

STUDY NOTE

Kinsman-redeemer. Hebrew: *go'el*, from *ga'al*, "to redeem." The law of Moses gives the nearest male relative the privilege or responsibility to be a *go'el*, to act for someone in trouble, danger, or need of vindication.

The *go'el* is a male relative who delivers or rescues (Genesis 48:16; Exodus 6:6); redeems property (Leviticus 27:9–25) or person (Leviticus 25:47–55); avenges the murder of a relative as a guiltless executioner (Numbers 35:9–34); and receives restitution for wrong done to a relative who has since died (Numbers 5:8).

3. To understand more about what "spread your covering" (3:9) means in the context of God's "covering," look up the following six verses. What do you learn about God's covering?

Ruth 2:12

Psalm 36:7

Psalm 57:1

Psalm 61:4

Psalm 91:4

Matthew 23:37

The image of God covering us with wings of protection is beautiful to think about. Imagine the Lord protecting you, covering you with His wings, carrying you on His pinions (part of a bird's wing). The security found in God's covering brings courage as we attempt to fly on our own. When a baby eagle is learning to fly, the mother drops the baby in the sky, then rescues the baby on her pinions and carries it safely. For many of us, our insecurity has kept us from "flying." Think about how Ruth's life became full of confidence and purpose because she trusted in the security not of her circumstances but of her Father's protection. Through her faith, His hand was outstretched to her. She went to God for her needs. He provided Naomi and Boaz as instruments of provision.

4. Ruth receives the promise of redemption from Boaz (Ruth 3:11) and a pledge for the future (3:13, 15). What are his promises?

5. Has God ever provided a "Boaz" in your life, someone He has appointed to care or be there for you?

6. Just as Boaz was used to redeem Ruth's life, God is Israel's and our Redeemer. Boaz redeemed with his resources; Jesus redeems us by giving His life. Reread Philippians 2:5–11, which we studied on Day 2, and reflect on the way Jesus became our Redeemer.

7. Read Ephesians 1:7 – 8 and fill in the blanks below.

In him we have _____ through his _____,
the _____, according to the
_____, which he lavished upon us, in all wisdom
and insight.

Christ redeemed us and, as we walk with Him, our virtue becomes His
arms offering redemption to all of mankind.

8. Write a prayer to your Redeemer, thanking Him for what He has done
for you. If you need to be redeemed from sin or an insecure situation, ask
Him for that redemption. Ask Him to cover you with His wings.

Day 5
Confidence

Hardships often prepare ordinary people for an extraordinary destiny.

C. S. Lewis

Ruth is an ordinary woman from a pagan background. Her hardships prepare
her for an extraordinary destiny! Her confidence is redeemed! Let's reflect on
the confidence that God builds into Ruth's and Naomi's lives.

1. Compare the way Naomi speaks of the Lord in Ruth 1:20 – 21 with the
way she speaks of Him in 2:20. What has changed? Why?

2. How does Naomi further grow in confidence in God as the story goes on?

3. Review Ruth 2:1 – 3:18. At what points does Ruth exercise confidence?

4. Does Ruth have about the same level of confidence from the beginning of the story to the end, or does she grow in confidence? What evidence do you see in the text?

There is no safer, more secure place for your life than trusting God, even in the dark places, because He already has a plan to see you through. As you bring your insecurity before Him, He brings strength and hope through His redeeming grace.

5. Read Psalm 91:1 – 2. How does this promise offer you confidence?

The Omnipotent Lord will shield all those who dwell with him, they shall remain under his care as guests under the protection of their host. In the most holy place the wings of the cherubim were the most conspicuous objects, and they probably suggested to the psalmist the expression here employed. Those who commune with God are safe with him, no evil can reach them, for the outstretched wings of his power and love cover them from all harm. This protection is constant — they abide under it, and it is all sufficient, for it is the shadow of the Almighty, whose omnipotence will surely screen them from all attack.

Charles Spurgeon

6. What is one area of your life where you want to grow in God-centered confidence?

All of us, at times, feel as if God has left us. Yet He is *with* us! We look around and wonder how God can be in our midst. We question God's providence because of our circumstances.

7. Read Habakkuk 3:17–19. After reading it once, insert your own circumstances into the words of the text. Pray this aloud to God.

8. Habakkuk has discovered a key to increasing his confidence. Where does he place his focus?

God can bring meaning and blessing to you in the most surprising ways. The Lord God is your strength. Rejoice in Him. He is the God of your salvation. He will make your feet like hinds' feet, and make you walk on high places.

God took Ruth's life and redeemed it for a great purpose—the lineage of Jesus. He can take your insecurity and fragility and do beyond what you can imagine.

SESSION 7

FROM INSIGNIFICANCE
TO COURAGE

ESTHER

Be strong and courageous. Do not fear or be in dread of them, for it is the LORD your God who goes with you. He will not leave you or forsake you.

Deuteronomy 31:6

EACH OF US LONGS TO FEEL SIGNIFICANT. We want our life to matter. Yet we often allow circumstances and status to define us. What would happen if we allowed God to courageously lead us with purpose? As Dr. Seuss said, "Oh, the places we would go!" Can you imagine the possibilities we have in Christ?

Esther, orphaned and under the guardianship of her cousin, Mordecai, had little sense of her true identity until God led her into the court of the Persian king to save the Jewish people. At first it seemed that she was no more than the pawn of a powerful man, but she discovered that no matter how things appear, God is in control. Yes, she was afraid, but prayer gave her courage to take action.

The courage we need to live significant lives may be beyond our own ability. Yet if we seek and receive courage from God, we can do what He is asking of us. Esther's life shows us the way.

WELCOME (5 minutes)

Before looking at Esther's life, take a minute to complete the following sentence, and then share your answer with the group:

The most courageous thing I've done recently is _____.

VIDEO: FROM INSIGNIFICANCE TO COURAGE (23 minutes)

Play the video segment for Session 7. As you watch, use the outline provided to follow along or to take notes on anything that stands out to you.

NOTES

When your real story encounters a real God, then anything is possible!

God is calling us to a life of significance for the kingdom.

God uses the least likely people to do mighty things for Him.

God took Esther's frightening and demeaning situation and used it to anoint her for something greater.

God had a plan to turn Esther from being the possession of the king into a woman of great purpose: to save her people.

Esther displayed a godly courage that came from one source alone.

Our moment will come when we are asked to step out of a place of insignificance and courageously stand for the King.

It's time for us to prepare:

- Tuck God's Word deep into our heart.
- Teach our children well.
- Fast and pray for our work in the kingdom.

Only God knows if we have come to the kingdom for such a time as this.

GROUP DISCUSSION

VIDEO DEBRIEF (5 minutes)

> If your group meets for two hours,
> allow 10 minutes for this discussion.

1. Which part of Sheila's teaching made the biggest impression on you?

INSIGNIFICANCE (10 minutes)

> If your group meets for two hours,
> allow 20 minutes for this discussion.

2. Read Esther 2:5–8. Describe what we know about Esther.

3. In contrast, what do we know about King Xerxes from Esther 1:1 – 12? Describe him and his lifestyle.

4. Why might Esther have felt insignificant when she was first taken to Xerxes' harem?

STUDY NOTES

Xerxes (Esther 1:1 NIV). Or "Ahasuerus" in ESV. He was king of Persia from 486 to 465 BC. (Esther became queen in about 479 BC.) The empire he inherited from his father reached from India to Sudan and included most of what we call the Middle East. The ancient Greek historian Herodotus portrayed him as a cruel narcissist. Herodotus wrote that when a storm destroyed a bridge that Xerxes was building, he ordered the water itself to be whipped three hundred times. The great banquet Xerxes gave for 180 days (Esther 1:1 – 9) was to display his wealth and glory.

Young women gathered in Susa (2:8). To find a new queen, Xerxes sent soldiers into the villages of his empire to round up young women for the king's harem. These women were taken by force. No Jewish woman would have volunteered to enter the king's harem. The harem itself was in the capital city, and the women would spend the rest of their lives within the harem walls, never seeing their families again.

OPTIONAL GROUP DISCUSSION *(10 minutes)*

DEMORALIZED

- What do you think it was like for a young woman, orphaned at the age of thirteen or fourteen, to enter the king's harem? Was it flattering, scary, degrading, honorable?
- What do you think it was like for her to "find favor" with the eunuch in charge of the harem (2:8–20)?
- Have you ever found yourself in a situation that you didn't expect and wondered how you got there? If so, describe this situation to the group.

COURAGE *(10 minutes)*

> *If your group meets for two hours,*
> *allow 20 minutes for this discussion.*

5. Read Esther 2:8–20. How does Esther demonstrate courage?

6. Why do you think Mordecai wants Esther to conceal her ethnic background from the king? What might it be like for her to do this?

STUDY NOTE

Kindred ... people (Esther 2:20). Esther did not deny her Jewish heritage, but she did not proclaim it because Mordecai had asked her not to do so. She was descended from Jews who had been exiled from Judah by the Babylonians in the previous century.

OPTIONAL GROUP DISCUSSION *(15 minutes)*

RISK

The king delighted in Esther. The Hebrew literally says, "She lifted up grace before his face" (2:17). Once he chose her as queen, her life seemed secure. She could have spent the rest of her life safe and pampered but with little true purpose. Then Mordecai interrupts her safe life with a risky challenge.

- Read Esther 3:1 – 4:14. Describe the challenge Esther faces. What does Mordecai ask her to do? Why is it dangerous?
- Read 4:13 – 14 again. What might be the consequences if Esther chooses cowardice instead of courage?
- "Who knows whether you have not come to the kingdom for such a time as this?" (4:14). How might Mordecai's words apply to you?

LIVING COURAGEOUSLY (10 minutes)

> *If your group meets for two hours,*
> *allow 30 minutes for this discussion.*

Courage is being scared to death but saddling up anyway.

John Wayne

7. Courage is the quality of mind or spirit that enables a person to face difficulty, danger, or pain in spite of fear. We can walk in courage because Jesus promises in Hebrews 13:5 that He will never leave us or forsake us.

   For what circumstance do you need to know that as you step out in courage, there is nothing to ultimately fear because Jesus will never leave you?

8. Has anything kept you from standing up in courage? If so, what?

9. Esther's courage is tested to the limit once she learns of Haman's plot to annihilate the Jews. After Mordecai challenges Esther to stand up for her people (see Esther 4:12–14), how does Esther respond (verses 15–17)? Why do you think she does this?

Prayer and fasting help us understand God's ways and take on His courage. Take some time to pray for courage. Esther did not attempt this undertaking alone. As Esther went to her people, whom can you enlist to pray for you?

Father, I desire to walk in courage and strength like Esther. In some moments I feel courageous, yet in other moments I am fearful. I give my fear to You, Jesus, trusting in Your promise that You will never leave me nor forsake me. God, You provide the power to do beyond what I am able. You took a young girl, exalted her to the position of queen, and asked her to risk her life by opposing a terrible plot. Take my life, Lord, my seemingly insignificant life, and make me into a woman standing courageously in You. In Jesus' name, Amen.

Personal Studies

Day 1
Significance

As women, we tend to base our significance on a variety of things other than what God says is true about us. This creates a roller-coaster life. We say to ourselves, "I would be the least likely to be picked for this or that." "I'm not good enough to ..." "If I attempt to do this and fail ..." We compare ourselves to others and always fall short.

The only place we can find true significance is in what God says is true. Esther's life displays God's sovereign purpose lived out through one who is least likely to save a people.

1. How do *you* evaluate your significance in this world? Is it based on your faith? On your status in this world? Of the criteria below, check the ones that pertain to you.

   ❑ Home location   ❑ Physical appearance
   ❑ Family background   ❑ Weight
   ❑ Religious involvement   ❑ Scholastic degrees
   ❑ Job status   ❑ Financial earning ability
   ❑ Relationship status   ❑ Social activity
   ❑ Position of influence   ❑ Social calendar
   ❑ Church attendance   ❑ Blessings in my life
   ❑ Consistent Bible reading   ❑ Sexual purity
   ❑ Ministry achievement   ❑ Career achievement

For many of us, our performance determines our value. The performance criteria may be religious or worldly, but in either case we aren't resting in our inherent value as daughters of God. Others base our significance on the world's status symbols. Esther's story defines significance not by what we have or what we do but by what God desires for our life and where He wants to take us.

2. Read Esther 2:5 – 18 again. In what things, other than her identity as God's daughter, might Esther have found her sense of significance and value?

STUDY NOTE

Favor (Esther 2:9, 17). In the Old Testament, the Hebrew word *hesed* is usually used for God's loving-kindness, steadfast love, or mercy toward His chosen people. This word is associated with God's covenant — His unbreakable promise of relationship — with His people. In 2:15; 5:2, 8; 7:3; and 8:5 a different word for favor is used. The story of Esther is not so much the story of a girl who is lucky enough to win favor with powerful men but the story of a God who graciously gives His favor to His people, even when they are imperfect people like Esther.

---

3. Esther was an orphan and a Jewish woman in a pagan empire. In a worldly sense, there was no reason she would be chosen to have influence on a king or be used for any great purpose of God. Look at your own life. Do you see yourself as significant to God, worthy to be chosen to do something special? Why or why not?

4. The truest thing about you is what God says about you. Read the following passages and write down the affirming truth mentioned in each one:

Ephesians 2:10

Hebrews 13:5–6

Luke 12:6–7

2 Peter 1:3

Romans 8:31–32

5. Choose one of the passages from question 4, and tell how it speaks to your own desire for identity and significance. How does it challenge the things that tempt you to doubt your worth?

Jesus came to announce to us that an identity based on success, popularity and power is a false identity—an illusion! Loudly and clearly he says: You are not what the world makes you; but you are children of God.

Henri J. M. Nouwen

Ask God to help you find your significance in Him.

Dear God, if I look at my life based on my own merit and background, it is confusing to believe that my life is significant to You or others. I've made mistakes, I've often been unrecognized, and I've failed when I have been recognized. I come to Your truth and understand that You and You alone make me righteous and give me an inheritance. I am loved by You, I am Your child, I am Your workmanship. Father, I want to embrace these truths, believing that I am valuable and significant in Your eyes. In Jesus' name, Amen.

DAY 2
COURAGE

Esther displayed a courage that came from one source alone.

Sheila Walsh

God calls us each to a life of courage. Our identity determines how we approach situations that require courage.

1. When have you done something courageous, taking action, even in a small way, despite your fear? Take some time to reflect on some courageous moments. When were they? What was the result?

2. Esther is married to an unpredictable and self-centered man. But that isn't the only danger she faces. Read Esther 3:1 – 11. Describe what you observe about Haman. What sort of man is he?

STUDY NOTES

Agagite (Esther 3:1). Haman was descended from Agag, the king of the Amalekites. Centuries before Esther's time, the Amalekites were so depraved and so repeatedly hostile to Israel that God told King Saul to defeat them and leave no captives alive. Saul infuriated the prophet Samuel by not killing King Agag (1 Samuel 15:1–33).

The king's gate (3:3). The gate of a city, palace, or fortress was where the governing officials and other citizens gathered to do commercial and legal business. Mordecai has a position as a minor government official (possibly through Esther's influence), so he sits with the other officials at the palace gate.

3. Read Esther 4:4–11. When Esther learns of the plot to kill the Jews, her first response is to avoid taking responsibility. How is it significant that courage doesn't come naturally to Esther? What does that say about the message of this story?

4. Read 4:12–14. How does Mordecai stir up Esther's courage?

5. Esther decides to put herself under God's protection, incorporating others to pursue God's direction as she approaches this challenge (4:15–17). Do you lean on God when faced with things beyond your ability? Do you

seek Him and rely on His presence and wisdom? Or are you more prone to one of these responses: (1) "I can't do anything. It's not my responsibility," or (2) "I'll take care of it. I can do it without help."

Wait for the LORD; be strong, and let your heart take courage; wait for the LORD!

Psalm 27:14

Take some time to wait on the Lord today. Bring to Him the things you fear and ask Him to strengthen your heart, to bring you courage. Align your heart with His, receiving courage and strength.

DAY 3
GOD IS WITH US

Esther is the only book in the Bible that doesn't mention God, yet His fingerprints are all over its pages. God promises He is with us. We may not see Him or hear His voice any more clearly than Esther does, but God assures us over and over again that He is with us wherever we go. When things seem out of control for Esther and Mordecai, when evil seems unavoidable, God is still in control of the whole story. He will triumph.

1. Is it sometimes difficult to remember that God is with you? When do you question His presence?

2. Read Esther 5:1 – 8 and Proverbs 21:1. On the third day, when the impression of God is fresh on her spirit, Esther presents herself to the king. What evidence do you see of God's presence at this moment?

STUDY NOTES

The king's heart (Proverbs 21:1). God controls the lives and actions even of kings, such as Nebuchadenezzar (Daniel 4:31 – 32, 34 – 35) and Cyrus (Isaiah 45:1 – 3; cf. Ezra 6:22).[12]

Court (Esther 5:1 – 2). Why doesn't Esther simply tell Xerxes about the plot against the Jews right here in his throne room? Why invite him to a feast? Possibly for privacy: The court and throne room are almost certainly full of courtiers and attendants. Some or even many may be Haman's supporters.

Feast (5:4). The Hebrew word for "feast" or "banquet" used here occurs twenty times in the book of Esther and only four times elsewhere in the Old Testament. Both Xerxes and Esther use feasts for political purposes, and the events of the story lie behind the Feast of Purim, which Jews today still celebrate each year.

---

3. Read Esther 5:1 – 7:10. Esther doesn't go to the king and immediately complain about Haman's plot. Describe step-by-step how she deals with the king and Haman.

4. Where do you see God's involvement in the events of 5:9–7:10?

5. We have the promise of God's presence, even when our circumstances don't appear that way. What assurance do the following passages give you?

    Proverbs 16:9

    Deuteronomy 31:6–8

6. Tragedy strikes, our security is threatened, relationships fail, circumstances let us down, and yet God is still with us. How does God's faithfulness to Esther give you courage as you face your own circumstances?

Thank God for being with you. Ask Him to help you trust Him even though you can't see Him.

Day 4
Pride

> Pride is ruthless, sleepless, an unsmiling concentration on self.
>
> *C. S. Lewis*

Pride is a high or inordinate opinion of one's own dignity, importance, merit, or superiority, whether as cherished in the mind or as displayed in bearing and conduct. Everything is about you. *Am I getting what I deserve? How does this make me look?* It is difficult to ignore the glaring pride of Haman in the story of Esther. The root of pride can take over a heart and begin to send out tendrils that destroy.

1. Look again at Esther 2:21 – 3:15. How does pride rear its head? What does Haman want that he doesn't get?

2. Haman reacts with anger and a desire for vengeance. Read Proverbs 11:2. Why do you suppose pride so often leads to disgrace?

Study Note

10,000 talents (Esther 3:9). An immense sum: 375 tons of silver. Haman may hope to recoup some of that money when the executioners seize the goods of the massacred Jews. Still, Matthew Henry says, "Proud and malicious men will not stick at the expenses of their revenge, nor spare any cost to gratify it."

3. Read Esther 6:1–13. Where do you see Haman's pride at work?

4. Have you seen pride rear its head in your life? If so, when? Is there an area where you feel superior to others? Or a time when you were angry because others didn't give you the respect you felt you deserved?

5. Has this pride led you into actions that were hurtful or irrational? If so, what were those actions? (They might be passive actions like withdrawing, sulking, or refusing to talk to someone.)

6. In Psalm 139:23–24, David prays, "Search me, O God, and know my heart! Try me and know my thoughts! And see if there be any grievous way in me, and lead me in the way everlasting!" This is a passage that leads us into revelation from God. Ask God to reveal any area of pride in your life.

Clothe yourselves, all of you, with humility toward one another, for "God opposes the proud but gives grace to the humble." Humble yourselves, therefore, under the mighty hand of God so that at the proper time he may exalt you.

1 Peter 5:5–6

183

A proud man is always looking down on things and people; and, of course, as long as you are looking down, you cannot see something that is above you.

C. S. Lewis

DAY 5
SUCH A TIME AS THIS

You will never need more than God can supply.

J. I. Packer

Although Esther's life begins with insignificance, the hand of God orchestrates events and raises up a woman to accomplish His purpose. The lack of religious background, the loss of parents, Jewish descent, exiled family — none of it matters compared to the providence of God.

Isn't it amazing that in a male-dominated society, filled with the pride of Haman and the narcissism of King Xerxes, God raises up a woman to become a major vehicle to save His people? Do you believe God can direct your life, accomplishing purposes beyond your own ability? Your story has been written (Psalm 139:16); are you willing to live it?

1. Read Isaiah 55:8–9. How was this passage true in Esther's life?

2. Based on all that you have learned about Esther in this session, make a timeline of her life events that led to God's ultimate purpose for her, starting with the fact that she was an orphan.

3. Take an inventory of your own life. What are some puzzling events that you are currently facing?

Who knows whether you have not come to the kingdom for such a time as this?

Esther 4:14

4. Now ask yourself the following questions in light of Esther 4:14. Is there a place in your life where God wants to work through you for "such a time as this"?

Where does He have you—even if it seems like a hard place or an ordinary place?

With whom does He have you?

What are you facing that could be turned around for good?

How might God use you in this place? (If you don't know, ask Him.)

5. We have promises as we live out the courageous calling of God. Write down the promise from each passage below.

Psalm 75:6–7

Ephesians 3:20

Romans 8:28

Ephesians 1:11

Be a woman of courage. Rise up! Only God knows if He may be preparing you for a unique work that only you can accomplish for "such a time as this." Ask God to reveal His ways and His plans for you. Ask Him for courage to walk in faith. Use the following psalm to pray.

The LORD is my light and my salvation;
    whom shall I fear?
The LORD is the stronghold of my life;
    of whom shall I be afraid?
When evildoers assail me
    to eat up my flesh,
my adversaries and foes,
    it is they who stumble and fall.

Though an army encamp against me,
    my heart shall not fear;
though war arise against me,
    yet I will be confident.
One thing have I asked of the LORD,
    that will I seek after:
that I may dwell in the house of the LORD
    all the days of my life,
to gaze upon the beauty of the LORD
    and to inquire in his temple.

Psalm 27:1–4

FROM DESPAIR
TO FAITH

SARAH

Now faith is the assurance of things hoped for, the conviction of things not seen.

Hebrews 11:1

HAVE YOU EVER BEEN CAUGHT in a situation that seemed impossible, and despair loomed around the corner? Sarah, a woman in the Old Testament, was filled with doubt and probably full of questions for God. She was childless and postmenopausal, yet God promised her husband, Abraham, that his descendants would be more than the stars.

All of us face circumstances that challenge our faith. We question God's promises and wonder about His timing. Sarah shows us how to walk with faith in the midst of despair.

WELCOME (5 *minutes*)

Give each person the opportunity to share the following in one sentence:

When have you walked by faith rather than by sight? (If you can't think of an obviously spiritual example, choose something ordinary. Even eating fast food without checking out the kitchen is an exercise in faith these days!)

VIDEO: FROM DESPAIR TO FAITH (20 *minutes*)

Play the video segment for Session 8. As you watch, use the outline provided to follow along or to take notes on anything that stands out to you.

NOTES

When you know exactly what is going to happen, you don't need faith.

Being a woman of faith doesn't mean that you never doubt or question.

Despair is the loss of hope in the mercy of God.

Despair can make us rationalize.

Getting ahead of God's plan can lead to suffering and despair.

Silence from God can sometimes feel like solitary confinement.

God sees who we will ultimately become.

Faith focuses not on what we feel or see but on God and what He has promised.

A life of faith is an unabashed focus on God as faithful.

GROUP DISCUSSION

VIDEO DEBRIEF (5 minutes)

> *If your group meets for two hours,*
> *allow 10 minutes for this discussion.*

1. What was most encouraging to you about Sheila's teaching?

PROMISE (10 minutes)

> *If your group meets for two hours,*
> *allow 20 minutes for this discussion.*

2. Read Genesis 12:1–3. What did God promise to Abraham?

3. What was Abraham's response in Genesis 12:4–5? See also Hebrews 11:8–10.

STUDY NOTES

A great nation (Genesis 12:2). At this time, Abraham and Sarah (called Abram and Sarai prior to Genesis 17) had no children. God's promise of blessing was fulfilled in Abraham's wealth (13:2; 24:35), God's presence (21:22), and fame (23:6; Isaiah 41:8). His descendants came years later through the birth of Isaac. At the time of his death, the only part of Canaan he owned was the cave where he was buried.

Haran ... Canaan (12:4 – 5). Abraham and Sarah came from Ur, a city on the Euphrates River in what is now Iraq (Genesis 11:27 – 32). With some of their relatives, they moved several hundred miles north along the Euphrates to Haran. When Abraham was seventy-five years old, they moved to Canaan, hundreds of miles southwest of Haran. Going to Canaan meant leaving the reliable water supply of the Euphrates and depending on rain in a land that had frequent droughts. It also meant leaving most of their relatives. The legal system of that culture provided few protections for individuals, so people largely relied on extended family for help and protection.

4. How did Abraham's response to God's promise affect Sarah?

5. What were some of the possible thoughts and feelings she might have had about a promise that was given not to her personally but to her husband?

OPTIONAL GROUP DISCUSSION (*15 minutes*)

ROOTS OF DESPAIR

- Have you ever been uprooted from all that was familiar to you? If so, what was your response?
- Childlessness led Sarah to despair. What are some of the circumstances today that can tempt you toward despair?

FAITH (10 MINUTES)

> *If your group meets for two hours,
> allow 20 minutes for this discussion.*

6. Define faith by putting Hebrews 11:1 into your own words. (Consider looking at several translations.)

7. Why do you suppose God cares so much about this process of learning to trust before seeing?

8. Think of a situation in your own life that has challenged your faith. How do you typically respond when you can't see God's plan?

Study Note

Covenant (Genesis 17:2). A covenant is an agreement between two parties, such as a marriage or a treaty. Usually both parties promise to do things. In Genesis 12 and 15, God does the promising. He promises Abraham land, descendants, and blessing. In response, He asks Abraham to go to the land and not take possession of it yet.

In Genesis 17, God repeats His promises. In response, He asks Abraham to "walk before me, and be blameless" (17:1) and to circumcise all males in his household (17:10).

Optional Group Discussion (15 minutes)

Waiting for the Promise

In the video Sheila says, "When you see exactly what is going to happen, you don't need faith." God continued to promise descendants, yet Sarah continued to be without children.

- Read Genesis 16:1–6. Where do you see Sarah's despair in her words? In her actions?
- How can we have faith when what we are promised and what we see are different? What enables a person to have faith?

Laughter (10 minutes)

9. Read Genesis 17:15–19 and 21:1–7. Abraham and Sarah have laughed in disbelief at God's promise. How does God have the last laugh in this story?

> ## Study Note
>
> **Isaac (Genesis 17:19; 21:3).** God says Sarah's son will be called Isaac, which in Hebrew means "he laughs." Initially, this is God's response when Abraham laughs at God's promise of a son in his old age (17:15–18). Later, Sarah too laughs at the promise, and God calls her out on it (18:9–15). Sarah refers to the laughter again when, after twenty-five years in Canaan, Sarah finally has a baby (21:1–7).

10. What are the one or two main things you've gained from this study of *The Storm Inside*? What are you grateful for?

11. As you end this study, how can the group pray for you?

Dear God, You alone are faithful to Your promises. Your word is true and never changing. I bring my doubt to You, these areas of my life where I question Your timing and wonder what You are trying to accomplish. I question if You know best. I wonder if You are still there. But I wait. Father, You promise that You are good to those who wait on You. In You I put my trust. In Jesus' name, Amen.

SESSION 8

PERSONAL STUDIES

DAY 1
DESPAIR

> Despair is the loss of hope in the mercy of God.
>
> *Sheila Walsh*

Sarah's life must have been filled with despair. As a barren woman, her heart was full of loss. Combine her loss with God's desire to make her husband the father of nations, and it's easy to understand why she lost hope. It's one thing to have loss but another when your loss directly affects the very thing God is calling your husband to do. Her value as a woman and as a wife is compromised.

1. Think about the greatest places of loss in your life. Write down a few of them.

2. Have you ever experienced a complete loss of hope? If so, when?

3. How did the loss affect other areas of your life?

4. Read Genesis 16:1–16. What did Sarah's despair move her to do?

5. What were the consequences for her? For Abraham? For Hagar? For Hagar's child?

STUDY NOTES

Dealt harshly (Genesis 16:6). From the Hebrew verb *'anah*, "to afflict, oppress, humble, try to force submission, punish or inflict pain upon."[13] This probably included physical beating to the point where Hagar fled, possibly to protect her life and the life of her unborn child.

Hagar (16:8). Sarah and Abraham only call her "my servant" or "your servant." God addresses her by name as a person, not just a role.

Submit (16:9). Again the root word is *'anah*. Amazingly, God asks Hagar to submit to whatever Sarah dishes out. God's purposes here aren't clear, but He could intend a season of spiritual growth for Hagar, a chance for Ishmael to know his father, and a time for Sarah and Abraham to experience the consequences of their bad choice. Later, God will allow Hagar and Ishmael to escape this bad situation.

6. Read Hebrews 11:11–12. Does it surprise you that after Sarah's despair caused such terrible pain, the writer of Hebrews can still call her a woman of faith? Why or why not?

7. What do you learn about God from this episode in Sarah's life?

8. When we get ahead of God's plan, this may lead to suffering. Have you ever experienced suffering as you stepped ahead of God's plan? If so, how has this suffering been your teacher?

9. What does Sarah's experience of despair and God's response say to you in your life? Write out a prayer to God in which you talk about what Sarah's story says to you.

Faith's most severe tests come not when we see nothing, but when we see a stunning array of evidence that seems to prove our faith vain.

Elisabeth Elliot

DAY 2
WAITING

"Wait on the Lord" is a constant refrain in the Psalms, and it is a necessary word, for God often keeps us waiting. He is not in such a hurry as we are, and it is not his way to give more light on the future than we need for action in the present, or to guide us more than one step at a time. When in doubt, do nothing, but continue to wait on God. When action is needed, light will come.

J. I. Packer

1. Have you experienced a time of waiting? What have been your various responses (in emotion and action) during this process?

2. After twenty-four years in Canaan, when Sarah is eighty-nine years old, God promises that "she shall become nations; kings of peoples shall come from her" (Genesis 17:16). Read 18:1–15. What does God promise here to Sarah?

STUDY NOTE

The LORD ... three men (Genesis 18:1–2). A visible manifestation of God in the Old Testament is called a *theophany*, a Greek term that means "appearance of [a] god." Here it seems that the Lord Himself appears to Abraham and Sarah along with two angels.

3. Laughter can express several different emotions, from happiness to scorn. What emotion(s) do you think lie behind Sarah's laughter here? Why does she laugh?

4. In verse 13, why do you suppose the Lord challenges Sarah's laughter? Why didn't He just let it go?

5. In verse 15, Sarah denies that she laughed. What does this say about her?

6. Do you find yourself wanting to laugh at God, as Sarah did? If so, why? If not, what do you think about Sarah's laughter?

7. Nothing is too difficult for God. Read Jeremiah 32:17. How does this verse provide comfort for you today?

8. How will you deal with waiting today? Talk with God about this.

Day 3
Faithful

> A life of faith is an unabashed focus on God as faithful.
>
> *Sheila Walsh*

Sarah's age and childlessness show absolutely no signs of a future filled with descendants. Yet God is faithful.

1. Have you questioned God's faithfulness? In the left column below, list times or events that have caused you to question Him. In the right column, describe how God has been faithful.

Insecure Area	God's Plans
Example: Loss of Job 5/2008	New Job 9/2009

2. Look up the verses below and describe God's faithfulness.

   Deuteronomy 7:9

   Psalm 36:5

   Psalm 119:90

   Psalm 100:5

   Taken as a whole, what do all these verses say about God's faithfulness?

STUDY NOTE

Faithful. Trustworthy, truthful, the quality of keeping promises.

---

3. The writer of Lamentations affirms God's faithfulness in the midst of terrible suffering. Read Lamentations 3:16–26. How does this poet describe his suffering?

4. What does he say about God's faithfulness in Lamentations 3:22–23?

5. How easy is it for you to be fully honest about pain and fully confident of God's faithfulness? If you tend to lean toward one or the other, which one do you lean toward? Why?

6. Reminding ourselves of God's faithfulness provides encouragement as we wait. Spend some time reflecting on your circumstances listed in question 1 and write out a prayer affirming God's faithfulness in the midst of them. Ask God to give you the faith to believe in His faithfulness.

Dear God, You promise to be faithful, and You have been faithful in the past, but my circumstances seem beyond Your ability. I bring this to You, God, and ask for the faith to believe. With You all things are possible. I step forward in faith, trusting because of who You are. In Jesus' name, Amen.

DAY 4
FAITH

Faith is defined in Hebrews 11, and there Sarah is listed as one of faith's heroes. At point, in desperation, she chose to place her faith in God and not herself.

1. Read Hebrews 11:1 – 26 to understand more clearly the value of faith, demonstrated by Sarah and others. According to verse 6, how does God describe the role of faith?

2. Why is it impossible to draw near to God without believing that those who seek Him will find Him?

3. Does that mean that wavering in our faith disqualifies us? Explain.

4. For Sarah, there is no way in her own power to produce offspring or increase Abraham's descendants. According to verses 11 – 12, what shifted in her focus as she lived out God's plans alongside Abraham?

STUDY NOTE

As good as dead (Romans 4:19). Because Abraham was 100 years old when Isaac was born, he counted his body "as good as dead." Faith does not refuse to face reality but looks beyond all difficulties to God and His promises.[14]

5. Hebrews 11:13 says, "These all died in faith, not having received the things promised, but having seen them and greeted them from afar, and having acknowledged that they were strangers and exiles on the earth." Sarah had a son before she died. Yet in what sense did she die in faith, not yet having received the things promised?

6. Is it enough for you to live your whole life not having received what has been promised you but seeing and greeting those things from afar? Explain.

7. Where do you need to shift your focus? Imagine your "barrenness" turned plentiful. Be specific. Can you turn your eyes toward God and the plenty He can bring?

8. Have you ever walked by faith? Describe the process and what you experienced. How did that journey change you?

As you close, pray to shift your focus away from yourself and toward God and His promises.

> *God, I stand before You, desiring to please You. Without faith it is impossible to please You. I shift my focus now on You, and not on my own ability. I desire to walk by faith, not by sight. Father, You are the God of the impossible. I place my faith in You today, trusting You to be and do beyond what I am able. In Jesus' name, Amen.*

DAY 5
FAITH IS NOT A FEELING

> Faith doth not come by feeling, but through faith arises much of holy feeling, and the more a man lives in the walk of faith, as a rule, the more will he feel and enjoy the light of God's countenance. Faith hath something firmer to stand upon than those ever-changing frames and feelings which, like the weather of our own sunless land, is fickle and frail, and changeth speedily from brightness into gloom.
>
> *Charles Spurgeon*

It is challenging to intentionally choose faith rather than rest on our feelings. Our feelings are real, rising up in passion and vigor. But when we allow our feelings to navigate our journey, we end up miles off course. Even then God is merciful and calls us back to faith over and over again. Sarah repeatedly encountered feelings that challenged her faith.

1. Review the details of Sarah's life, listing times that presented opportunities to respond with faith or feelings. Note how she responded and why.

Genesis 12

Genesis 16

Genesis 17:15–21

Genesis 18:9–15

Genesis 21:1–7

STUDY NOTE

Say that you are my sister (Genesis 12:13). If Pharaoh were to add Sarah to his harem while knowing that she was Abraham's wife, he would have to kill Abraham first.

---

2. What determines how you respond to your circumstances? Check the items below that apply to you, and add any additional ones to the list.

❑ Fear   ❑ Refocusing
❑ Facts   ❑ Hormones
❑ Disbelief   ❑ Other (name it):
❑ Faith
❑ Impatience   _____
❑ Joy   ❑ Other (name it):
❑ God's faithfulness
❑ Bad mood   _____
                            ❑ Other (name it):

                            _____

Faith, in the sense in which I am here using the word, is the art of holding on to things your reason has once accepted, in spite of your changing moods.

C. S. Lewis

3. From the checklist in question 2, do you notice anything that creates a response leading to faith rather than your feelings? What is it?

If our eyes are focused on ourselves and our circumstances, we never press beyond into the arena of faith. Faith steps into the supernatural. Feelings trap us in our circumstances and limitations. Faith calls on the power of God. Feelings can distance us from that power. Faith enables us to view life through God's eyes.

4. Looking back over the eight weeks of this study, what are the key insights you would like to apply to your life?

5. In what ways do you see growth in yourself, even if it feels tiny?

6. As you move forward, which areas do you most want to continue praying about? Or, to put it another way, what is the Lord currently working on in your life: love, hope, joy, strength, rest, family, courage, faith?

7. Finally, as you think back over this study, what are you grateful for? Spend some time expressing that gratefulness to God in a written prayer.

Faith focuses not on what we feel or see but on God and what He has promised. It's important to be honest with ourselves about our feelings, even unattractive ones like shame, disappointment, fear, regret, insecurity, or despair. God doesn't want us to stuff our feelings and pretend they're not there. He wants us to have the faith to go to Him with those feelings, and to at least a few people we trust, and pursue His grace to be transformed. God hasn't promised us pain-free lives. Rather, He has promised us that, like the Samaritan woman and Mary Magdalene, like Rahab and Sarah, like the woman with the issue of blood and Hannah, like Ruth and Esther, we can become loving, courageous, faithful women no matter what happens. We don't have to be overwhelmed by the storm inside. God is faithful. He is the one who is calling His daughters all around the world to rise up in His name, standing strong on the Rock who is Christ Jesus, our Lord!

About the Author

~

SHEILA WALSH IS A COMMUNICATOR, Bible teacher, and best-selling author with more than four million books sold. A featured speaker with Women of Faith, Sheila has reached more than three and a half million women by artistically combining honesty, vulnerability, and humor with God's Word.

Sheila is the author of the bestselling memoir *Honestly* and the Gold Medallion nominee *The Heartache No One Sees*. Her most recent books are *Beautiful Things Happen When a Woman Trusts God*, *The Shelter of God's Promises*, and *The Storm Inside*. She has also written a novel, *Angel Song*, and has written several children's books, including *Gigi, God's Little Princess*, which has a companion video series that has won the national Retailer's Choice award twice and is the most popular Christian brand for young girls in the United States.

Sheila cohosted *The 700 Club* and her own show, *Heart to Heart with Sheila Walsh*. She is currently completing her master's in theology and lives in Dallas, Texas, with her husband, Barry; son, Christian; and two little dogs, Belle and Tink.

Visit her website at www.sheilawalsh.com
Facebook: www.facebook.com/sheilawalshconnects
Twitter: @sheilawalsh / www.twitter.com/sheilawalsh
Instagram: @sheilawalsh1

NOTES

1. *NASB Study Bible*, study notes (Grand Rapids: Zondervan, 1999), 1523.
2. Ibid., 1734.
3. Ibid., 1734.
4. Walter W. Wessel, *Expositor's Bible Commentary*, vol. 8, *Mark* (Grand Rapids: Zondervan, 1984), 662.
5. *NASB Study Bible*, study notes, 1547.
6. Merrill C. Tenney, *Expositor's Bible Commentary*, vol. 9, *John* (Grand Rapids: Zondervan, 1981), 183.
7. A. Skevington Wood, *Expositor's Bible Commentary*, vol. 11, *Ephesians* (Grand Rapids: Zondervan, 1981), 85.
8. *NASB Study Bible*, study notes, 1414.
9. Willem A. VanGemeren, *Expositor's Bible Commentary*, vol. 5, *Psalms* (Grand Rapids: Zondervan, 1991), 330ff.
10. Ibid., 420ff.
11. *NASB Study Bible*, study notes, 353.
12. Ibid., 920.
13. Leonard J. Coppes, *'anah, Theological Wordbook of the Old Testament*, ed. R. Laird Harris, Gleason L. Archer, and Bruce K. Waltke (Chicago: Moody, 1980), 1652.
14. *NASB Study Bible*, study notes, 1640.

No matter *the* storm,
God knows, God cares, *and*
He is always there

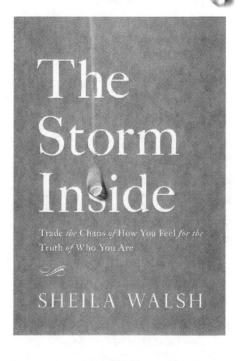

The
Storm
Inside

Trade *the* Chaos *of* How You Feel *for the*
Truth *of* Who You Are

SHEILA WALSH

Available wherever books *and* ebooks are sold.

You know God's promises, but are they for you, are they for now, are they for this? If you look to your circumstances alone, it may seem that God has forgotten you. But He hasn't. He can't. And He wouldn't even if He could. God is the only promise maker who is always a promise keeper. And God's promises will never fail you!

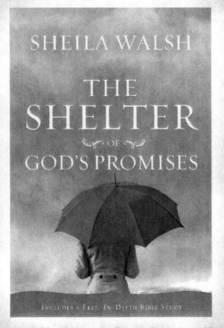

Available wherever books and ebooks are sold.

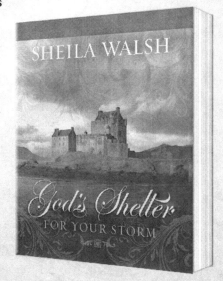

Time for bed!

Every little princess needs to fall asleep
with God's promises on her heart.

(978-1-4003-2293-0)

106 devotions, prayers, scriptures
and inspirational thoughts with a
sparkly cover that girls will love

Check out *the* brand new

www.SheilaWalsh.com

Get info *on her* upcoming events, books, *and* social media!